The Ultimate Morning
Study Companion
German Edition

MICHAEL D. YOUNG

ISBN:1491275588
ISBN-13:9781491275580

DEDICATION

To all those who serve the Lord with all heart, might, mind and strength.

Unit 1
>
> Grammar: Nouns and Articles
> Pronunciation: The Alphabet
> Culture: Greeting Others
> Vocabulary: Prayer

Unit 2
>
> Grammar: Regular Verbs
> Pronunciation: The Letter Z
> Culture: Shopping
> Vocabulary: Shopping

Unit 3
>
> Grammar: Irregular Verbs
> Pronunciation: The Letter S
> Culture: Eating at a Home
> Vocabulary: Numbers and Shapes

Unit 4
>
> Grammar: Questions and Commands
> Pronunciation: The Letter W
> Culture: Restaurants
> Vocabulary: Restaurant

Unit 5
>
> Grammar: Accusative Case
> Pronunciation: The Letter V
> Culture: Public Transportation
> Vocabulary: Public Transportation

Unit 6
>
> Grammar: Adjectives
> Pronunciation: The Letter Q
> Culture: Driving
> Vocabulary: In the Car

Unit 7
>
> Grammar: Conjunctions
> Pronunciation: The Letter R
> Culture: Holidays
> Vocabulary: At Church

Unit 8
>
> Grammar: Dative Case
> Pronunciation: The Letter J
> Culture: Religion
> Vocabulary: Sight-Seeing/Holidays

Unit 17
>Grammar: Da and Wo Compounds
>Pronunciation: The Letter D
>Culture: German School System
>Vocabulary: Free time activities

Unit 18
>Grammar: Reflexive Verbs
>Pronunciation: The Combination CH
>Culture: German Architecture
>Vocabulary: Adjectives

Unit 19
>Grammar: Relative Clauses
>Pronunciation: Final –E vs. Final -ER
>Culture: German Regional Accents
>Vocabulary: Body

Unit 20
>Grammar: Als, wenn, wann
>Pronunciation: M and N
>Culture: Famous German Speakers
>Vocabulary: The City

Unit 21
>Grammar: Passive Voice
>Pronunciation: GN, NG, and PF
>Culture: German Sports
>Vocabulary: Weather

Unit 22
>Grammar: Weak Masculine Nouns
>Pronunciation: CK and CHS
>Culture: German Art
>Vocabulary: Animals and Nature

Unit 23
>Grammar: Infinities plus zu
>Pronunciation: The Letter G
>Culture: German Literature
>Vocabulary: On the Phone

Unit 24
>Grammar: Subjunctive II
>Pronunciation: The Letter Y
>Culture: German Music
>Vocabulary: Professions

German Missionary Terms

Deutsch	English
das Evangelium	the Gospel
dif Taufe	the baptism
die Kirche	the church
das Priestertum	the priesthood
der Missionar	the missionary
der Tempel	the temple
der Heilige Geist	the Holy Ghost
der Heiland	the Savior
der Erlöser	the Redeemer
die Schriften	the Scriptures
das Namensschild	the nametag
der Himmlische Vater	the Heavenly Father

das Gebet	the prayer
der Glauben	the faith
die Umkehr	the repentence
im Namen Jesu Christi	in the name of Jesus Christ
das Kollegium	the quorum
der Apostel	the apostle
der Jünger	the disciple
der Bischof	the bishop
die Gemeinde	the bishop
die Gemeinde	the ward
der Zweig	the branch
der Präsident	the president
die Präsident	the president
die Präsidentschaft	the presidency
die Bischofschaft	the bishopric

die Keuschheit	the chastity
der Zehnten	the tithing
die Bibel	the Bible
das Buch Mormon	the Book of Mormon
Die Lehre und Bündnisse	The Doctrine and Covenants
Die Köstliche Perle	the Pearl of Great Price
die Offenbarung	the revelation
der Prophet	the prophet
das Gesangbuch	the hymnbook
die Ansprache	the talk
das Zeugnis	the testimony
die Berufung	the calling
die Abendmahlsversamml	the sacrament meeting

ung	
der Gott	the God
die Sünde	the sin
das Sühnopfer	the Atonement
das Opfer	the sacrifice
das Gebiet	the area
die Zone	the zone
der Distriksleiter	the district leader
der Zonenleiter	the zone leader
die Konfirmierung	the confirmation
die Begabung	the endowment
die Ehe	the marriage
die Ewigkeit	the eternity
die ewige Ehe	the eternal marriage
das Celestiale Reich	the Celestial Kingdom

der Abfall	the Apostasy
die Schriftstelle	the scripture
die Glaubensartikel	the Articles of Faith
der Engel	the angel
der Teufel	the devil
bis ans Ende ausharren	enduring to the end
die Erhöhung	the exaltation
die Erste Vision	the First Vision
die Wiederherstellung	the Restoration
der Schlüssel	the key
das Abendmahl	the sacrament
der Segen	the blessing
die Geisterwelt	the Spirit World
das Gefängnis	the prison
der Pfahl	the stake

das Heimlehren	home teaching
das Wort der Weisheit	the World of Wisdom
Junge Männer	Young Men
Junge Damen	Young Women
der Chor	the choir
die Generalkonferenz	the General Conference
die Demut	the humility
die Gnade	the grace
das Wasser	the water
das Brot	the bread
der Tod	the death
die Auferstehung	the resurrection

Parts of Prayer/Teile des Gebets

1. Lieber Himmlischer Vater…

2. Wir danken dir…

3. Wir bitten dich (um)

4. Im Namen Jesu Christi, amen.

Michael D. Young

Scritpure Mastery

Old Testament

Moses 1:39

Moses 7:18

Genesis 1:26-7

Genesis 39:9

Abraham 3:22-3

Exodus 20:3-17

Exodus 33:11

Leviticus 19:18

Deuteronomy 7:3-4

Joshua 1:8

Joshua 24:15

1 Samuel 16:7

Job 19:25-6

Psalms 24:3-4

Proverbs 3:5-6

Isaiah 1:18

Isaiah 29:13-4

Isaiah 53:3-5

Isaiah 55:8-9

Jeremiah 16:16

Ezekiel 37:15-7

Daniel 2:44-5

Amos 3:7

Malachi 3:8-10

Malachi 4:5-6

New Testament

Matthew 5:14-6

Matthew 6:24

Matthew 16:15-9

Matthew 25:40

Luke 24:36-9

John 3:5

John 7:17

John 10:16

John 14:15

John 17:3

Acts 7:55-6

Romans 1:16

1 Corinthians 10:13

1 Corinthians 15:20-2

1 Corinthians 15:29

1 Corinthians 15:40-2

Ephesians 4:11-4

2 Thessalonians 2:1-3

2 Timothy 3:1-5

2 Timothy 3:16-7

Hebrews 5:4

James 1:5-6

James 2:17-8

Revelation 14:6-7

Revelation 20:12-3

Book of Mormon

1 Nephi 3:7

1 Nephi 19:23

2 Nephi 2:25

2 Nephi 2:27

2 Nephi 9:28-9

2 Nephi 28:7-9

2 Nephi 32:3

2 Nephi 32:8-9

Jacob 2:18-9

Mosiah 2:17

Mosiah 3:19

Mosiah 4:30

Alma 32:21

Alma 34:32-4

Alma 37:6-7

Alma 37:35

Alma 41:10

Helaman 5:12

3 Nephi 11:29

3 Nephi 27:27

Ether 12:6

Ether 12:27

Moroni 7:16-7

Moroni 7:45

Moroni 10:4-5

Doctrine and Covenants

D&C 1:37-8

D&C 8:2-3

D&C 10:5

D&C 14:7

D&C 18:10, 15-6

D&C 19:16-9

D&C 25:12

D&C 58:26-7

D&C 58:42-3

D&C 59:9-10

D&C 64:23

D&C 64:9-11

D&C 76:22-4

D&C 82:3

D&C 82:10

D&C 84:33-9

D&C 88:123-4

D&C 89:18-21

D&C 121:34-6

D&C 130:18-9

D&C 130:20-1

D&C 130:22-3

D&C 131:1-4

D&C 137:7-10

Joseph Smith History 1:15-20

The Articles of Faith

of The Church of Jesus Christ of Latter-day Saints

1. We believe in God, the Eternal Father, and in His Son, Jesus Christ, and in the Holy Ghost.
2. We believe that men will be punished for their own sins, and not for Adam's transgression.
3. We believe that through the Atonement of Christ, all mankind may be saved, by obedience to the laws and ordinances of the Gospel.
4. We believe that the first principles and ordinances of the Gospel are: first, Faith in the Lord Jesus Christ; second, Repentance; third, Baptism by immersion for the remission of

sins; fourth, Laying on of hands for the gift of the Holy Ghost.

5. We believe that a man must be called of God, by prophecy, and by the laying on of hands by those who are in authority, to preach the Gospel and administer in the ordinances thereof.

6. We believe in the same organization that existed in the Primitive Church, namely, apostles, prophets, pastors, teachers, evangelists, and so forth.

7. We believe in the gift of tongues, prophecy, revelation, visions, healing, interpretation of tongues, and so forth.

8. We believe the Bible to be the word of God as far as it is translated correctly; we also believe

the Book of Mormon to be the word of God.

9. We believe all that God has revealed, all that He does now reveal, and we believe that He will yet reveal many great and important things pertaining to the Kingdom of God.

10. We believe in the literal gathering of Israel and in the restoration of the Ten Tribes; that Zion (the New Jerusalem) will be built upon the American continent; that Christ will reign personally upon the earth; and, that the earth will be renewed and receive its paradisiacal glory.

11. We claim the privilege of worshiping Almighty God according to the dictates of our own

conscience, and allow all men the same privilege, let them worship how, where, or what they may.

12. We believe in being subject to kings, presidents, rulers, and magistrates, in obeying, honoring, and sustaining the law.

13. We believe in being honest, true, chaste, benevolent, virtuous, and in doing good to all men; indeed, we may say that we follow the admonition of Paul—We believe all things, we hope all things, we have endured many things, and hope to be able to endure all things. If there is anything virtuous, lovely, or of good report or praiseworthy, we seek after these things.

Joseph Smith

Die Glaubensartikel

Der Kirche Jesu Christi Der Heiligen Der Letzten Tage

History of the Church (Geschichte der Kirche), Band 4, S. 535–541

1 Wir aglauben an Gott, den Ewigen Vater, und an seinen Sohn, Jesus Christus, und an den Heiligen Geist.

2 Wir glauben, daß der Mensch für seine eigenen Sünden bestraft werden wird und nicht für die Übertretung Adams.

3 Wir glauben, daß durch das Sühnopfer Christi alle Menschen errettet werden können, indem sie die Gesetze und Verordnungen des Evangeliums befolgen.

4 Wir glauben, daß die ersten

Grundsätze und Verordnungen des Evangeliums sind: erstens der Glaube an den Herrn Jesus Christus; zweitens die Umkehr; drittens die Taufe durch Untertauchen zur Sündenvergebung; viertens das Händeauflegen zur Gabe des Heiligen Geistes.

5 Wir glauben, daß man durch Prophezeiung und das Händeauflegen derer, die Vollmacht dazu haben, von Gott berufen werden muß, um das Evangelium zu predigen und seine heiligen Handlungen zu vollziehen.

6 Wir glauben an die gleiche Organisation, wie sie in der Urkirche bestanden hat, nämlich Apostel, Propheten, Hirten, Lehrer, Evangelisten usw.

7 Wir glauben an die Gabe der

Zungenrede, Prophezeiung, Offenbarung, der Visionen, der Heilung, Auslegung der Zungenrede usw.

8 Wir glauben, daß die Bibel, soweit richtig übersetzt, das Wort Gottes ist; wir glauben auch, daß das Buch Mormon das Wort Gottes ist.

9 Wir glauben alles, was Gott offenbart hat, und alles, was er jetzt offenbart; und wir glauben, daß er noch viel Großes und Wichtiges offenbaren wird, was das Reich Gottes betrifft.

10 Wir glauben an die buchstäbliche Sammlung Israels und die Wiederherstellung der Zehn Stämme, daß Zion (das Neue Jerusalem) auf dem amerikanischen Kontinent errichtet werden wird, daß Christus persönlich

auf der Erde regieren wird und daß die Erde erneuert werden und ihre paradiesische Herrlichkeit empfangen wird.

11 Wir beanspruchen das Recht, den Allmächtigen Gott zu verehren, wie es uns das eigene Gewissen gebietet, und gestehen allen Menschen das gleiche Recht zu, mögen sie verehren, wie oder wo oder was sie wollen.

12 Wir glauben, daß es recht ist, Königen, Präsidenten, Herrschern und Obrigkeiten untertan zu sein und dem Gesetz zu gehorchen, es zu achten und für es einzutreten.

13 Wir glauben, daß es recht ist, ehrlich, treu, keusch, gütig und tugendhaft zu sein und allen Menschen Gutes zu tun; ja, wir können sagen, daß

wir der Ermahnung des Paulus folgen—
wir glauben alles, wir hoffen alles, wir
haben viel ertragen und hoffen, alles
ertragen zu können. Wenn es etwas
Tugendhaftes oder Liebenswertes gibt,
wenn etwas guten Klang hat oder
lobenswert ist, so trachten wir danach.

Joseph Smith

The Family: A Proclamation to the World

We, the First Presidency and the Council of the Twelve Apostles of The Church of Jesus Christ of Latter-day Saints, solemnly proclaim that marriage between a man and a woman is ordained of God and that the family is central to the Creator's plan for the eternal destiny of His children.

All human beings—male and female—are created in the image of God. Each is a beloved spirit son or daughter of heavenly parents, and, as such, each has a divine nature and destiny. Gender is an essential characteristic of individual premortal, mortal, and eternal identity and purpose.

In the premortal realm, spirit sons and daughters knew and worshipped God as their Eternal Father and accepted His plan by which His children could obtain a physical body and gain earthly experience to progress toward perfection and ultimately realize their divine destiny as heirs of eternal life. The divine plan of happiness enables family relationships to be perpetuated beyond the grave. Sacred ordinances and covenants available in holy temples make it possible for individuals to return to the presence of God and for families to be united eternally.

The first commandment that God gave to Adam and Eve pertained to their potential for parenthood as husband and wife. We declare that God's commandment for His children to multiply and replenish the earth remains in force. We further declare that God has commanded that the sacred powers of procreation are to be employed only between man and woman, lawfully wedded as husband and wife.

We declare the means by which mortal life is created to be divinely appointed. We affirm the sanctity of life and of its importance in God's eternal plan.

Husband and wife have a solemn responsibility to love and care for each other and for their children. "Children are an heritage of the Lord" (Psalm 127:3). Parents have a sacred duty to rear their children in love and righteousness, to provide for their physical and spiritual needs, and to teach them to love and serve one another, observe the commandments of God, and be law-abiding citizens wherever they live. Husbands and wives—mothers and fathers—will be held accountable before God for the discharge of these obligations.

The family is ordained of God. Marriage between man and woman is essential to His eternal plan. Children are entitled to birth within the bonds of matrimony, and to be reared by a father and a mother who honor marital vows with complete fidelity. Happiness in family life is most likely to be achieved when founded upon the teachings of the Lord Jesus Christ. Successful marriages and families are established and maintained on principles of faith, prayer, repentance, forgiveness, respect, love, compassion, work, and wholesome recreational activities. By divine design, fathers are to preside over their families in love and righteousness and are responsible to provide the necessities of life and protection for their families. Mothers are primarily responsible for the nurture of their children. In these sacred responsibilities, fathers and mothers are obligated to help one another as equal partners. Disability, death, or other circumstances may necessitate individual adaptation. Extended families should lend support when needed.

We warn that individuals who violate covenants of chastity, who abuse spouse or offspring, or who fail to fulfill family responsibilities will one day stand accountable before God. Further, we warn that the disintegration of the family will bring upon individuals, communities, and nations the calamities foretold by ancient and modern prophets.

We call upon responsible citizens and officers of government everywhere to promote those measures designed to maintain and strengthen the family as the fundamental unit of society.

Die Familie: Eine Proklamation an die Welt

Die Erste Präsidentschaft und der Rat der Zwölf Apostel der Kirche Jesu Christi der Heiligen der Letzten Tage

Wir, die Erste Präsidentschaft und der Rat der Zwölf Apostel der Kirche Jesu Christi der Heiligen der Letzten Tage, verkünden feierlich, dass die Ehe zwischen Mann und Frau von Gott verordnet ist und dass im Plan des Schöpfers für die ewige Bestimmung seiner Kinder die Familie im Mittelpunkt steht.

Alle Menschen — Mann und Frau — sind als Abbild Gottes erschaffen. Jeder Mensch ist ein geliebter Geistsohn beziehungsweise eine geliebte Geisttochter himmlischer Eltern und hat dadurch ein göttliches Wesen und eine göttliche Bestimmung.Das Geschlecht ist ein wesentliches Merkmal der individuellen vorirdischen, irdischen und ewigen Identität und Lebensbestimmung.

Im vorirdischen Dasein kannten und verehrten die Geistsöhne und -töchter ihren ewigen Vater und nahmen seinen Plan an; nach diesem Plan konnten sie einen physischen Körper erhalten und die Erfahrungen des irdischen Lebens machen, um sich auf die Vollkommenheit hin weiterzuentwickeln und letztlich als Erben ewigen Lebens ihre göttliche Bestimmung zu verwirklichen. Der göttliche Plan des Glücklichseins macht es möglich, dass die Familienbeziehungen über das Grab hinaus Bestand haben. Die heiligen Handlungen und Bündnisse, die im heiligen Tempel vollzogen werden können, ermöglichen es dem Einzelnen, in die Gegenwart Gottes zurückzukehren, und der Familie, auf ewig vereint zu sein.

Das erste Gebot, das Gott Adam und Eva gab, bezog sich darauf, dass sie als Ehemann und Ehefrau Eltern werden konnten. Wir verkünden, dass Gottes Gebot für seine Kinder, sich zu vermehren und die Erde zu bevölkern, noch immer in Kraft ist. Weiterhin verkünden wir, dass Gott geboten hat, dass die heilige Fortpflanzungskraft nur zwischen einem Mann und einer Frau angewandt werden darf, die rechtmäßig miteinander verheiratet sind.

Wir verkünden, dass die Art und Weise, wie sterbliches Leben erschaffen werden soll, von Gott so festgelegt ist. Wir bekräftigen, dass das Leben heilig und in Gottes ewigem Plan von wesentlicher Bedeutung ist.

Mann und Frau tragen die feierliche Verantwortung, einander und ihre Kinder zu lieben und zu umsorgen. "Kinder sind eine Gabe des Herrn." (Psalm 127:3.) Die Eltern haben die heilige Pflicht, ihre Kinder in Liebe und Rechtschaffenheit zu erziehen, für ihre physischen und geistigen Bedürfnisse zu sorgen, sie zu lehren, dass sie einander lieben und einander dienen, die Gebote Gottes befolgen und gesetzestreue Bürger sein sollen, wo immer sie leben. Mann und Frau — Vater und Mutter — werden vor Gott darüber Rechenschaft ablegen müssen, wie sie diesen Verpflichtungen nachgekommen sind.

Die Familie ist von Gott eingerichtet. Die Ehe zwischen Mann und Frau ist wesentlich für seinen ewigen Plan. Das Kind hat ein Recht darauf, im Bund der Ehe geboren zu werden und in der Obhut eines Vaters und einer Mutter aufzuwachsen, die den Ehebund in völliger Treue einhalten. Ein glückliches Familienleben kann am ehesten erreicht werden, wenn die Lehren des Herrn Jesus Christus seine Grundlage sind. Erfolgreiche Ehen und Familien gründen und sichern ihren Bestand auf den Prinzipien Glaube, Gebet, Umkehr, Vergebungsbereitschaft, gegenseitige Achtung, Liebe, Mitgefühl, Arbeit und sinnvolle Freizeitgestaltung. Gott hat es so vorgesehen, dass der Vater in Liebe und Rechtschaffenheit über die Familie präsidiert und dass er die Pflicht hat, dafür zu sorgen, dass die Familie alles hat, was sie zum Leben und für ihren Schutz braucht.Die Mutter ist in erster Linie für das Umsorgen und die Erziehung der Kinder zuständig. Vater und Mutter müssen einander in diesen heiligen Aufgaben als gleichwertige Partner zur Seite stehen. Behinderung, Tod oder sonstige Umstände mögen eine individuelle Anpassung erforderlich machen. Bei Bedarf leisten die übrigen Verwandten Hilfe.

Wir weisen warnend darauf hin, dass jemand, der die Bündnisse der Keuschheit verletzt, der seinen Ehepartner oder seine Kinder misshandelt oder seinen familiären Verpflichtungen nicht nachkommt, eines Tages vor Gott Rechenschaft ablegen muss. Weiter warnen wir davor, dass der Zerfall der Familie Unheil über die einzelnen Menschen, die Gemeinwesen und die Nationen bringen wird, wie es in alter und neuer Zeit von den Propheten vorhergesagt worden ist.

Wir rufen die verantwortungsbewussten Bürger und Regierungsvertreter in aller Welt auf, solche Maßnahmenzu fördern, die darauf ausgerichtet sind, die Familie als Grundeinheit der Gesellschaft zu bewahren und zu stärken.

The Living Christ

As we commemorate the birth of Jesus Christ two millennia ago, we offer our testimony of the reality of His matchless life and the infinite virtue of His great atoning sacrifice. None other has had so profound an influence upon all who have lived and will yet live upon the earth.

He was the Great Jehovah of the Old Testament, the Messiah of the New. Under the direction of His Father, He was the creator of the earth. "All things were made by him; and without him was not any thing made that was made" (John 1:3). Though sinless, He was baptized to fulfill all righteousness. He "went about doing good" (Acts 10:38), yet was despised for it. His gospel was a message of peace and goodwill. He entreated all to follow His example. He walked the roads of Palestine, healing the sick, causing the blind to see, and raising the dead. He taught the truths of eternity, the reality of our premortal existence, the purpose of our life on earth, and the potential for the sons and daughters of God in the life to come.

He instituted the sacrament as a reminder of His great atoning sacrifice. He was arrested and condemned on spurious charges, convicted to satisfy a mob, and sentenced to die on Calvary's cross. He gave His life to atone for the sins of all mankind. His was a great vicarious gift in behalf of all who would ever live upon the earth.

We solemnly testify that His life, which is central to all human history, neither began in Bethlehem nor concluded on Calvary. He was the Firstborn of the Father, the Only Begotten Son in the flesh, the Redeemer of the world.

He rose from the grave to "become the firstfruits of them that slept" (1 Corinthians 15:20). As Risen Lord, He visited among those He had loved in life. He also ministered among His "other sheep" (John 10:16) in ancient America. In the modern world, He and His Father appeared to the boy Joseph Smith, ushering in the long-promised "dispensation of the fulness of times" (Ephesians 1:10).

Of the Living Christ, the Prophet Joseph wrote: "His eyes were as a flame of fire; the hair of his head was white like the pure snow; his countenance shone above the brightness of the sun; and his voice was as the sound of the rushing of great waters, even the voice of Jehovah, saying:

"I am the first and the last; I am he who liveth, I am he who was slain; I am your advocate with the Father" (D&C 110:3–4).

Of Him the Prophet also declared: "And now,

after the many testimonies which have been given of him, this is the testimony, last of all, which we give of him: That he lives!

"For we saw him, even on the right hand of God; and we heard the voice bearing record that he is the Only Begotten of the Father—

"That by him, and through him, and of him, the worlds are and were created, and the inhabitants thereof are begotten sons and daughters unto God" (D&C 76:22–24).

We declare in words of solemnity that His priesthood and His Church have been restored upon the earth—"built upon the foundation of . . . apostles and prophets, Jesus Christ himself being the chief corner stone" (Ephesians 2:20).

We testify that He will someday return to earth. "And the glory of the Lord shall be revealed, and all flesh shall see it together" (Isaiah 40:5). He will rule as King of Kings and reign as Lord of Lords, and every knee shall bend and every tongue shall speak in worship before Him. Each of us will stand to be judged of Him according to our works and the desires of our hearts.

We bear testimony, as His duly ordained Apostles—that Jesus is the Living Christ, the immortal Son of God. He is the great King

Immanuel, who stands today on the right hand of His Father. He is the light, the life, and the hope of the world. His way is the path that leads to happiness in this life and eternal life in the world to come. God be thanked for the matchless gift of His divine Son.

Der Lebendige Christus

Wir gedenken in diesem Jahr der Geburt Jesu Christivor zweitausend Jahren und geben Zeugnis von der Realität seines unvergleichlichen Lebens und der unendlichen Macht seines großen Sühnopfers. Niemand sonst hat so großen Einfluss auf alle Menschen, die schon gelebthaben und noch leben werden.

Er war der erhabene Jahwe des Alten Testaments und derMessias des Neuen Testaments. Auf Weisung seines Vaterserschuf er die Erde. "Alles ist durch das Wort geworden, undohne das Wort wurde nichts, was geworden ist." (Johannes 1:3.) Er war ohne Sünde, aber er ließ sich doch taufen, um die Gerechtigkeit ganz zu erfüllen. Er zog umher und tat Gutes (siehe Apostelgeschichte 10:38) und wurde doch dafür verachtet. Sein Evangelium war die Botschaft vom Frieden für die Menschen seiner Gnade. Er forderte alle eindringlich auf, seinem Beispiel nachzueifern. Er wandelte auf den Straßen Palästinas, heilte die Kranken, machte die Blinden sehend und weckte die Toten auf. Er lehrte die Wahrheiten der Ewigkeit und sprach von unserem Vorherdasein, dem Zweck des Erdenlebens und den Möglichkeiten, die den Söhnen und Töchtern Gottesim zukünftigen Leben offen stehen.

Er führte das Abendmahl ein, das an sein großes Sühnopfer erinnern soll. Er wurde gefangen genommen und auf Grund von falschen Anschuldigungen angeklagt. Er wurde für schuldig befunden, damit der Pöbel Ruhe gab, und zum Tod am Kreuz auf dem Kalvarienberg verurteilt. Er gab sein Leben hin, um für die Sünden aller Menschen zu sühnen. Er war die große Gabe, die stellvertretend für alle Menschen dargebracht wurde, die je auf der Erde leben sollten.

Wir bezeugen feierlich, dass sein Leben, das ja den zentralen Punkt der Menschheitsgeschichte bildet, weder in Betlehem begann noch auf dem Kalvarienberg endete. Er war der Erstgeborene des Vaters, der einziggezeugte Sohn im Fleisch, der Erlöser der Welt.

Er ist aus dem Grab auferstanden — als "der Erste derEntschlafenen" (1 Korinther 15:20). Als auferstandener Herr

erschien er denen, die er während seines Erdenlebens geliebt hatte. Außerdem diente er seinen anderen Schafen (siehe Johannes 10:16) im alten Amerika. In der Neuzeit erschienen er und sein Vater dem jungen Joseph Smith und leiteten damit die lange verheißene "Fülle der Zeiten" ein (siehe Epheser 1:10).

Der Prophet Joseph schrieb über den

lebendigen Christus: "Seine Augen waren wie eine Feuerflamme, sein Haupthaar war weiß wie reiner Schnee, sein Antlitz leuchtete heller als der Glanz der Sonne, und seine Stimme tönte wie das Rauschen großer Gewässer, ja, die Stimme Jehovas, die sprach: "Ich bin der Erste und der Letzte; ich bin der, der lebt, ich binder, der getötet worden ist; ich bin euer Fürsprecher beim Vater." (LuB 110:3,4.)

Außerdem sagte der Prophet über ihn: "Und nun, nach denvielen Zeugnissen, die von ihm gegeben worden sind, ist dies, als letztes von allen, das Zeugnis, das wir geben, nämlich: Er lebt! Denn wir haben ihn gesehen, ja, zur rechten Hand Gottes; und wir haben die Stimme Zeugnis geben hören, dass er der Einziggezeugte des Vaters ist, dass von ihm und durch ihn und aus ihm die Welten sind und erschaffen worden sind und dass ihre Bewohner für Gott gezeugte Söhne und Töchter sind." (LuB 76:22-24.)

Wir verkünden feierlich, dass sein Priestertum und seine Kirche auf der Erde wiederhergestellt worden sind—"auf das Fundament der Apostel und Propheten gebaut; der Schlussstein ist Christus Jesus selbst" (Epheser 2:20).

Wir bezeugen, dass er eines Tages zur Erde zurückkehren wird. "Dann offenbart sich die

Herrlichkeit des Herrn, alle Sterblichen werden sie sehen." (Jesaja 40:5.) Dann regiert er als König der Könige und herrscht als Herr der Herren, und jedes Knie muss sich beugen und jede Zunge ihn preisen.

Alle Menschen werden dann vor dem Herrn stehen, um gemäß ihren Taten und den Wünschen ihres Herzens gerichtet zu werden.

Als seine rechtmäßig ordinierten Apostel bezeugen wir, dass Jesus der lebendige Messias ist, der unsterbliche Sohn Gottes. Er ist der große König Immanuel, der heute zur Rechten des Vaters steht. Er ist das Licht, das Leben und die Hoffnung der Welt. Sein Weg ist der Pfad, der zum Glücklichsein hier auf der Erde und zu ewigem Leben in der zukünftigen Welt führt. Gott sei gedankt für diese unvergleichliche Gabe, nämlich dafür, dass er uns seinen Sohn geschenkt hat.

Mission Milestones:

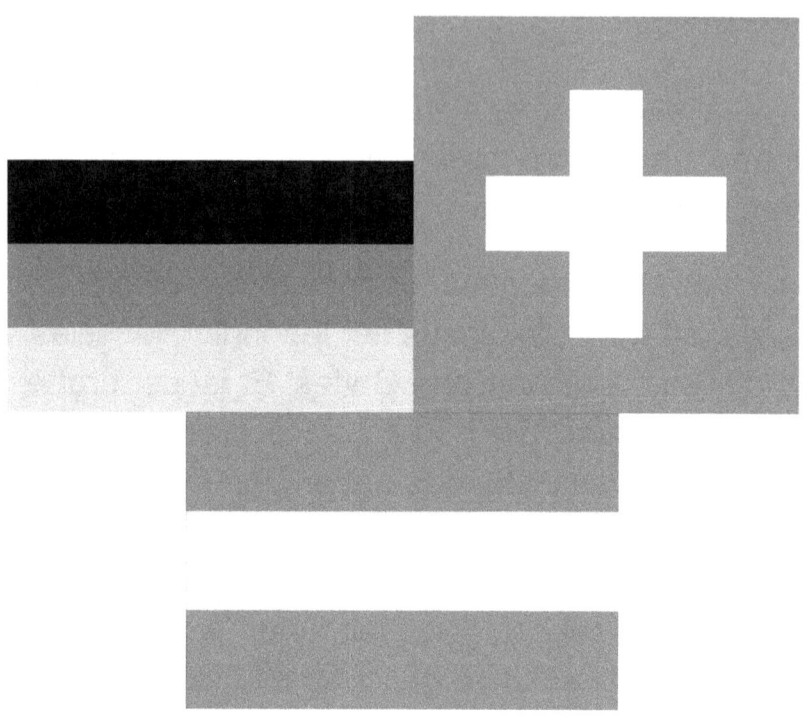

Firsts:

- Make first street contact.

  _____

- Make your first contact at the door.

  _____

- Have your first appointment.

  _____

- Have your first eating appointment.

  _____

- Do your first service project.

  _____

- Have aless-active appointment.

  _____

- Have your first baptismal date.

  _____

- Have your first baptism.

  _____

Food:

- Eat a Döner.

  _____

- Eat a Lamachun (Turkish pizza)

  _____

- Eat Bratwurst and a Weißwurst

  _____

- Buy something from a street vendor.

  _____

- Try a Wienerschniztel.

  _____

- Try Spaghettieis

  _____

- Order something from a local bakery.

  _____

- Try Rotkohl.

  _____

- Try Knödel.

  _____

- Try Spätzle

  _____

- Try Rouladen.

  _____

- Try a new kind of Ritter Sport.

  _____

- Try a Kinder Surprise Egg.

  _____

- Try Sauerkraut.

  _____

- Try Currywurst.

  _____

- Try Marzipan.

  _____

- Try Lebkuchen

  _____

- Try white Spargel.

  _____

- Have a piece of Black Forest Cake.

  _____

- Avoiding eating an alcoholic candy.

  _____

- Try a Berliner.

  _____

- Try Müsli.

  _____

- Try Leberwurst on bread.

  _____

- Drink an Apfelschorle.

  _____

- Drink a cup of peppermint tea.

  _____

- Try a new kind of Fanta.

  _____

- Try Fondue.

  _____

- Try Raclette.

  _____

- Try Sprudelwasser.

  _____

- Try a Bretzel.

  _____

Sights:

- Visit a castle.

  _____

- Visit ruins other than a castle.

  _____

- Visit a department store.

  _____

- Ride on a train.

  _____

- Visit an Altstadt

  _____

- Visit a supermarket.

  _____

- Visit an open-air market.

_____

- Visit an American fast food chain.

_____

- Visit a museum.

_____

- Visit a monument.

_____

- Visit a Christmas Market.

_____

- Visit a cathedral.

_____

- Mail something a local post office.

_____

- Eat a meal at a sit-down restaurant.

_____

Picture Opportunities:

Take a picture including:

- A train station.

_____

- A castle.

_____

- A post office.

_____

- A department store.

_____

- A multilingual advertisement.

  _____

- A river.

  _____

- Mountains.

  _____

- Your apartment.

  _____

- A tall building.

  _____

- A really old building.

  _____

- A pedestrian zone.

  _____

- A non-LDS church.

  _____

- An LDS church.

  _____

- A church member.

  _____

- An investigator.

  _____

- A restaurant.

  _____

- A funny street name.

  _____

- A funny name on a doorbell.

  _____

•A bus and a train.

_____

•A street sign.

_____

•Someone with a crazy hairstyle/color.

_____

•Someone wearing something funny.

_____

Weird and Wild Stuff:

•Find a non-member American.

_____

•Play a German board game.

_____

•Learn a song in German.

_____

•Use music in an appointment.

_____

•Play sports with the locals.

_____

•Memorize a poem in German.

_____

•Memorize a scripture in German.

_____

•Bear your testimony in German.

_____

•Sing in a special musical number.

_____

False Friends

Because German and English are related langauges, many words sound similar. This makes learning the language a bit easier.

German	English
der Vater	the father
die Mutter	the mother
der Bruder	the brother
die Schwester	the sister
der Onkel	the uncle
der Hund	the hound (dog)
die Lampe	the lamp
das Haus	the house
die Maus	the mouse

There are, however, a group of words called "false friends", which are words that sound like they might be related to an English word, but actually have a different meaning. Knowing to look out for these will help you avoid embarrassing mistakes. The following is a list of a few common examples, though this list is by no means comprehensive.

Nouns

German Definition	English	False
die Angel	the fishing pole	the angel
die Fabrik	the factory	the fabric
die Pension	the small hotel	the pension
der Pickel	the pimple	the pickle
der Stuhl	the chair	the stool
die Hose	the pants	the hose
der Hut	the hat	the hut
das Kissen	the pillow	the kiss
das Gift	the poison	the gift
der Mist	the manure	the mist
der Kohl	the cabbage	the coal
die Uhr	the clock	the hour
der Roman	the novel	the roman
das Bad	the bath	bad
die Kraft	the strength	the craft
der Chef	the boss	the chef
der Dom	the cathedral	the dome
die Dose	the can	the dose

das Gymnasium	the high school	the gym
die Hochschule	college	the high school
die Kantine	the cafeteria	the cantine
die List	the cunning	the list
das Menü	the daily special	the menu
die Peperoni	chili peppers	peperoni
der Rat	the advice	the rat

Other Words and Phrases

German	English	False Definition
eventuell	maybe	eventually
fast	almost	fast
streng	strict	strong
hohl	hollow	hole
ich will	I want	I will
winken	to wave	to wink
bald	soon	bald
still	quiet	still
brav	well-behaved	brave
groß	big	gross
die Wand	the wall	the wand

The following is a list of useful words that will help you sound more like a native speaker. See if you can work them in to your conversation.

German	English
immer	always
nie	never
nimmer	never
vielleicht	maybe
ab und zu	now and then
bestimmt	definitely
oft	often
jedoch	however
obwohl	although
manchmal	sometimes
mindestens	at least
total	totally
endlich	finally
höchstens	at most
nochmal	again
normalerweise	usually

schon	already
zum Beispiel (z.B.)	for example
glücklicherweise	luckily, fortunately
natürlich	naturally
jetzt	now
später	later
plötzlich	suddenly
fast	almost
zuerst	first
überall	everyall
jeder	everyone
nirgendwo	nowhere
dringend	urgent
leider	unfortunately
irgendwo	somewhere
irgendwann	sometime

German Abbreviations:

The following are common abbreviations or Abkürzungen that you will see and hear.

German		**English**	
Abb.	Abbildung	Illus.	Illustration
Abf.	Abfahrt	Dep.	departure
Abs.	Absender	---	return address
Abt.	Abteilung	Dept.	department
a.D.	außer Dienst	ret.	retired
AG	Aktiengesellschaft	Inc.	Incorperated
a.M	am Main	---	on the Main (river)
Ank.	Ankunft	---	arrival
b.	bei	---	with/near/care of
Bd.	Band	Vol.	volume
Betr.	Betreff	Re:	regarding
Bhf.	Bahnhof	---	train station
BRD	Bundesrepublik Deutschland	FRG	Federal Republic of Germany
b.w.	bitte wenden	over	please turn over
d. Ä.	der Ältere	Sr.	senior
DB	Deutsche Bahn	---	German Rail
DDR	Deutsche Demokratische Rep.	GDR	German Democratic Rep.

DFB	Deutscher Fußballbund	---	German Soccer Association
d.h.	das heißt	i.e.	that is
d.J.	der Jüngere	Jr.	junior
EU	Europäische Union	EU	European Union
ev.	evangelisch	---	protestant
Fam.	Familie	---	family
FC	Fußball Club	---	Soccer Club
Fr.	Frau	Mrs.	Mrs.
geb.	geboren	b.	born
Gebr.	Gebrüder	Bros.	brothers
gegr.	gegründet	est.	established
Ges.	Gesellschaft	Co.	company
gest.	gestorben	d.	died
ggf.	gegenfalls	---	if required
GmbH	Gesellshaft mit beschränkter Haftung	Ltd.	limited liability co.
Hbf.	Hauptbahnhof	---	main train station
Hr.	Herr	Mr.	Mr.
IC	Intercityzug	---	intercity train
ICE	Intercitzy-Expresszug	---	high-speed train
i.J.	im Jahre	---	in the year
Kap.	Kapitel	ch.	chapter

kath.	katholisch	---	catholic
LKW	Lastkraftwagen	---	truck
MfG	Mit freundlichen Grüßen	---	sincerely
MwSt.	Mehrwertsteuer	VAT	value-added tax
n. Chr.	nach Christus	AD	anno domini
Nr.	Nummer	Num.	number
NS	Nachschrift	PS	post script
ÖBB	Österreichische Bundesbahnen	---	Austrian Railways
PKW	Personenkraftwagen	---	car
Pl.	Platz	---	place
PS	Pferdstärke	HP	horsepower
s.a	siehe auch	---	see also
s.o.	siehe oben	---	see above
s.u.	siehe unter	---	see below
Str.	Straße	st.	street
tägl.	täglich	---	daily
TÜV	Technische Überwachungsverein	DMV	DMV
U	U-Bahn	S	Subway
usw.	und so weiter	etc.	et cetera
v.Chr.	vor Christus	BC	before Christ
v.H.	vom Hundert	%	percent

WC	das WC	---	restroom
z.B.	zum Beispiel	e.g.	for example
z.Hd.	zu Handen	attn:	attention of

Abbreviations for Days of the Week

German   **English**

So.	Sonntag	Sun.	Sunday
Mo.	Montag	Mon.	Monday
Di.	Dienstag	Tue.	Tuesday
Mi.	Mittwoch	Wed.	Wednesday
Do.	Donnerstag	Thurs.	Thursday
Fr.	Freitag	Fri.	Friday
Sa.	Samstag.	Sat	Saturday

German Movie Ratings

dF, dtF deutsche Fassung = German dubbed version
k.A. keine Angabe = not rated, unrated, no information
FSF Freiwillige Selbstkontrolle Fernsehen = German TV rating board
FSK Freiwillige Selbstkontrolle der Filmwirtschaft = German film rating board
FSK 6, FSK ab 6 rated age 6 and up (More at the FSK site - in German.)
o.A. ohne Altersbeschränkung = approved for all ages, no age limit
OF Originalfassung = original-language version
OmU Originalfassung mit Untertiteln = orig. lang. with subtitles
SW, s/w schwarz/weiß = black & white

- **Ohne Altersbeschränkung (FSK 0)**: no age restriction (white sign)
- **Freigegeben ab 6 Jahren (FSK 6)**: no children younger than 6 years admitted (yellow sign)
- **Freigegeben ab 12 Jahren (FSK 12)**: children 12 or older admitted, children between 6 and 11 only when accompanied by parent or a legal guardian (green sign)
- **Freigegeben ab 16 Jahren (FSK 16)**: children 16 or older admitted, nobody under this age admitted (blue sign)
- **Keine Jugendfreigabe (FSK 18)**: "no youth admitted", only adults. (red sign)

- **Infoprogramm** or **Lehrprogramm**: "educational programming". This rating is not issued by the FSK, but may be self-applied to films seeking to educate their audience (e.g. documentaries, instructional films, etc.), provided they do not contain any material "evidently harmful to the development of children and youths". Films with this rating may be sold without any age restriction.

Major German Political Parties

CDU: Christliche Demokratische Union Deutschlands: Christian Democratic Union of Germany

CSU: Christlich-Soziale Union in Bayern: Christian Social Union of Bavaria

SPD: Sozialdemokratische Partei Deutschlands: Social Democratic Party of Germany

FDP: Freie Demokratische Partei: Free Democratic Party

LINKE: Die Linke: The Left

GRÜNE: Die Grüne: The Greens

There are similar parties in both Austria and Switzerland.

Grammar: Nouns and Articles

The Worth of Nouns is Great

The first thing you need to know about nouns is that they are always capitalized. In the English, we only capitalize the important ones, such as names of places and people. In German, however, any person, place, or thing deserves a big letter. This makes nouns easier to identify and it is an important rule to follow that does not have any exceptions.

English	German
the missionary	der Missionar
the bicycle	das Fahrrad
the book	das Buch
the door	die Tür
the appointment	der Termin
the car	das Auto

Three Choices for *the*

While the noun rule might be a bit easier than English, the way Germans use the word *the* might take some practice. There are three basic ways to say *the: **der, die** and **das.*** In addition, these three basic words have different forms depending on how they are used in a sentence. Remember that all forms of *the* start with the letter D.

How do you decide? In this case, you have to ask what gender the noun you are describing is. At first, you might think, nouns like *man* and woman have a gender, but about words like *table* or *fork*? In this case, gender is not taken in a literal sense, but only as a grammar term. Everything is assigned one of three grammatical genders, and it is something you just have to memorize about a word when you learn it. In fact, knife, fork and spoon are each a different grammatical gender.

The three genders are:

Masculine: use the article **der**

Feminine: use the article **die**

Neuter: use the article **das**

The good news is, that things that have a natural gender, tend to have the same grammatical gender:

English	German
the man	**der** Mann
the woman	**die** Frau
the boy	**der** Junge

The bad news is, that inanimate objects often do not have a rule to figure out which one of the genders they take. Look at the following example:

English	German
the knife	**das** Messer
the fork	**die** Gabel
the spoon	**der** Löffel

So, when you sit down to dinner, the silverware in front of you represents all three grammatical genders. It can be confusing, so I recommend that you learn the article for each noun along with the noun. After a while, you will start getting an ear for it, and at the end of the day, if you say the wrong article when talking to someone, they will still understand what you mean. Don't be embarrassed if Germans once in a while correct your articles.

Pronunciation: The Alphabet

Even though you are learning a new language, you're not going to have to learn a new alphabet, at least not a whole new one—just a few letters, and only one of those looks complete foreign to English speakers.

German uses all of the letters of the English alphabet plus four letters unique to the German alphabet. Many of the letter names sound similar to their English counterparts, though many of them make different sounds. The names of the letters are all mostly similar, but there are a few tricky ones. Pay special attention to the names of vowels, because they can be easily mixed up.

Let's take a look at the names and sounds of the letters in the German alphabet. An example word is given for each letter. The letters that are much different from their English counterparts are underlined.

A (ah) = Apfel

B (beh) = Boot

C (ceh) = Computer

D (deh) = Drachen

E (eh) = Elefant

F (ehf) = Fuchs

G (geh) = Glas

H (ha) = Haus

I (ee) = Insel

J (jot) = Jaguar, sounds like an English Y

K (kah) = Katze

L (el) = Löwe

M (em) = Mädchen

N (en) = Nadel

O (oh) = Orange

P (peh) = Pfirsich

Q (koo) = Qualle, sounds like the combination KV

R (er) = Rose, always said rolled on the tongue or back of throat

S (ess) = Suppe, sounds like an English Z

T (teh) = Trompete

U (oo) = Uhr

V (fau) = Vater, sounds like an English F

W (veh) = Würfel, sounds like an English V

X (iks) = Xylophon

Y (ypsilon) = Yacht

<u>Z (zett) = Zebra, sounds like the combination of TS</u>

You may have seen German words that have umlaut vowels. The umlaut is the name of the double dots that some German verbs can take. These letters can be some of the hardest for English speakers to master, because they correspond to sounds that English speakers do not usually make. If you need help with these, ask a native German speaker to demonstrate and pay close attention to how they shape their lips to make these sounds. The three vowels that can take an umlaut are a, o, and u. You will never see an I or an E with an umlaut.

Ä (ah umlaut) = Äpfel

Ö (oh umlaut) = Ökonom

Ü (oo umlaut) = Übermut

The final letter that you'll run into is a strange one for English speakers. It doesn't have an uppercase or lowercase form and its use is dying out in many cases. This letter is called the Eszett and it looks like the Greek letter beta or a variation on the English capital letter B. The Eszett is the same as writing SS. Remember that having only one S usually sounds like the English letter Z.

ß (Eszett) = Straße, sounds like the English letter S

The rules about when to use ß and when to use SS has changed over time. You will still see ß on many street signs, but many Germans avoid using ß. Currently, the rule is to use ß after a long vowel, such as in the word Straße, but not after a short vowel, such as in the word Gasse. Also use ß after diphthongs, which mean two vowels in a row.

The Eszett is gradually being used less and less, though you still should know how and when to use it.

Culture: Greetings and Farewells

Greetings

When you greet people in Germany, you'll need to keep in mind what time of day it is. In the morning, people often great each other with "Guten Morgen". In the afternoon, you will hear "Guten Tag" and in the evening "Guten Abend." You will often hear people leave of the "Guten" and just say "Morgen!" or "Tag!" Only use "Gute Nacht!" right before bedtime.

A simple "Hallo" will often do, though different regions of Germany, Austria and Switzerland have their own greetings. When greeting someone on the phone, many people simply say their last name, such as "Müller" or "Hurst". They might also say "Hallo, hier spricht…" and then their name. Here is a sampling you might hear:

Greeting	Where Heard
Moin!/Moin Moin!	Northern Germany
Grüß dich!	Germany
Grüß Gott!	Southern Germany, Austria
Grützi/Grützi miteinand!	Switzerland
Servus!	Austria, Bavaria

Once is Enough

Once you greet someone once during a day, you generally don't need to do it again unless a long time has passed. If you shake someone's hand to greet them, you don't generally shake it again on the same day or you might get a polite "Wir haben schon." (We have already.) This is especially important to remember at church meetings where you will probably see members more than once. One handshake will do!

Also when shaking hands with someone, be sure not to cross with someone shaking hands in the other direction. Many Germans are superstitious about doing this because it creates the sign of the swastika.

Farewells

There are many ways to bid farewell to someone in German. In formal situations, you might want to go with Auf Wiedersehen, but in informal situations, a simple "Tschüß!" will do. In some regions, you might even hear people use "Ciao!" Here are some others you might hear:

German	English
Schönen Tag noch!	Have a nice day!
Schönes Wochenende!	Have a good weekend!

Bis bald!	See you soon!
Bis morgen!	See you tomorrow!
Alles Gute!	All the best!
Viel Glück!	Good luck!
Mach's gut!	Take care!

When speaking to someone on the telephone, you generally use the farewell "Auf Wiederhören" which literally means "Until I hear you again". Saying "Auf Wiedersehen" would not be accurate because it means "Until I see you again".

How's It Going?

In the United States, it is common to hear people greet each other with the question "How's it going?" or "How are you?" This is not as common among German speakers, and unlike many people in the United States who often give a casual answer, German speakers will actually tell you exactly how they doing whether that be good or bad. If they are sick and feel like they need to throw up, they might just let you know that. It is fine to occasionally ask someone how they are doing, but you should not make it your greeting of choice, especially when greeting strangers at the door or on the streets.

Vocabulary: Prayer

Nouns:

German	English
das Gebet	the prayer
der Herr	the Lord
der Sohn	the son
die Segnung	the blessing
der Tag	the day
das Essen	the food
die Kirche	the church
das Sühnopfer	the Atonement
der Prophet	the prophet
die Missionare	the missionaries
der Erfolg	the success
die Kirche	the church
die Familie	the family
der Untersucher	the investigator
die Gesundheit	the health

die Hilfe	the help
der Geist	the spirit
der Mitarbeiter	the companion
die Gelegenheit	the oppurtunity

Verbs:

German	English
beten	to pray
danken	to thank
bitten	to ask
segnen	to bless
fragen	to ask a question
sagen	to say
helfen	to help
leiten	to lead
schützen	to protect
vergeben	to forgive
stärken	to strengthen
hören	to hear

Phrases:

German	English
German	**English**
Wir danken dir für…	We thank thee for…
We bitten dich um…	We ask thee for…
Im Namen Jesu Christi	In the name of Jesus Christ
Lieber Himmlischer Vater…	Dear Heavenly Father…
Bitte, segne…	Please bless…
Hilfe uns…	Help us…

Unit 2

Regular Verbs

A regular verb is a verb that acts like you would expect it to act. Like a good missionary, regular verbs don't break any of the rules.

Just like in English, verbs change their endings depending on the subject of the sentence. This process is called **conjugation**. Compare the following two sentences in English:

I talk to the investigator.   He talk**s** to the investigator.

You might be accused of sounding like a caveman if you said something like "He talk to the investigator." Making sure that you put the proper endings on your German verbs is just as important.

While English verbs usually have only two forms, German verbs have a great variety. These endings are *--e,- st, -t,* and *–en*. Which one you choose depends on the subject. Let's look at some examples using the regular verb *spielen* (to play).

To conjugate the verb *spielen*, you first have to drop the –en on the end of the verb and then add the correct ending, which might even be to add the *–en* back.

Add *–e* if the subject is *ich* (I).

Ich spiele Fußball.

I am playing soccer.

Add *–st* if the subject is *du*. (you-informal)

Du spielst Fußball.

You are playing soccer. (informal)

Add *–t* if the subject is *er/sie/es*. (he/she/it)

Er/Sie/Es spielt Fußball.

He/She/It is playing soccer.

Also add –t if the subject is ihr (you all-informal)

Ihr spielt Fußball.

You all are playing soccer.

Add –en if the subject is *wir* or *Sie/sie*. (we or you-formal/they)

Wir spielen Fußball.

We are playing soccer.

Sie* spielen Fußball.

You (formal) are playing soccer.

They are playing soccer.

*Sometimes you have to figure out the meaning of the word Sie from the context, especially in spoken

German. With a capital S, "Sie" means "you-formal", and with a lowercase S, "sie" can mean either "she" or "they".

Pronunciation: The Letter Z

The letter Z never sounds like it does in English. While it is a pretty rare letter in English, it is much more common in German, so you need to become familiar with the way to say it.

The letter Z makes a sound like the English combination TS. There really aren't many English words with these sounds, so it might take you a little practice. (It is similar to the final sound in the English words *nets* or *cats*.) You can also think of it as the sound a lawn sprinkler makes if that helps you. Mastering Z will help you sound a lot more like a native German speaker.

Z at the Beginning

German	English
der Zoo	the zoo
das Zimmer	the room
der Zucker	the sugar
die Ziege	the goat
der Zahn	the tooth
die Zeit	the time
die Zwiebel	the onion

zehn	ten
zwölf	twelve
zwanzig	twenty
zusammen	together
zurück	back

Z in the Middle

German	**English**
duzend	dozen
die Pizza	the pizza
die Abkürzung	the abbreviation
sitzen	to sit
setzen	to set
benutzen	to use
schmelzen	to melt
der Weizen	the wheat
das Flugzeug	the airplane
das Fahrzeug	the vehicle
der Arzt	the doctor

Z at the End

German	English
das Netz	the net
schwarz	black
kurz	short
der Schutz	the defense
das Herz	the heart
das Erz	the ore
der Schmerz	the pain
der Pelz	the fur

Culture: Shopping and Sending Mail

Shopping in German-speaking countries in many ways is very similar to the United States. They still have large Supermarkets and department stores such as Karstadt. In some areas, especially in smaller villages, the residents rely more on smaller neighborhood stores such as bakeries and butcher shops for their daily needs.

Some common grocery stores in German-speaking countries include Aldi, Liedel, Netto, Hofer, Kaiser, Globus Handelshof, Kaufland, Metro and Real. One of the first things you might notice when you enter one of these supermarkets, is that most of the time the carts will require you to place a coin in them in order to unlock them. The coin is returned when you place the cart back in its stall. This keeps shopping carts from going lost and encourages customers to return their carts when they are done.

Most grocery stores do not accept credit cards, but will accept debit cards linked to a European account.

You can often return you empty glass or plastic bottles (Leergut) to groceries stores for a small refund on each one.

Another difference about most German grocery stores is that the store does not provide free paper or plastic bags. Either you will have to purchase disposable bags at the time of purchase, or purchase studier, reusable bags to bring and use every time. You will usually not see designated baggers who will put your items in the bags for you, nor will the cashier usually do this. Make sure you plan accordingly and do your part so that you do not hold up other customers in line.

Do not expect to see many of the same brands that you see in the United States in German-speaking countries. In fact, you will see some products that you cannot find in the US and vice versa. For example, in German-speaking countries, you will see cartons of what is called "H-milk" which has been pasteurized to the point that it does not require refrigeration. You will also see a product called quark, which is similar to Greek yogurt.

You will have a much harder time, however, finding a store that will sell you peanut butter. Instead, you will find hazelnut spreads such as Nutella. Though you will find many kinds of carbonated drinks, including many familiar brands, you will not find many stores that sell root beer, because many Europeans think that it tastes more like medicine.

Many grocery stores will have an entire section devoted to different kinds of candy. Here you will most likely not find any American brands such as

Hershey's, but instead will find a host of European brands of chocolate such as Milka, Kinder, Ferreo, and Lindt-Sprüngli. Instead of finding peanuts in chocolate, you will most often taste hazelnuts.

A fun chocolate product is called Kinder Eggs, which are hollow chocolate eggs made out of milk and white chocolate. Inside is a plastic container that holds some sort of prize—usually a figurine or a toy that you can put together. There are often sets of figures based on movies, TV shows, or other popular cultural icons for fans to collect.

When you see a price tag, what you see is what you have to pay. The value-added-tax or Mehrwertsteuer/Umsatzsteuer, is already included of the listed price of any item.

There are certain conditions in which a non-European taking a product out of the European Union can apply for a refund of the value-added tax. This is a complicated process and must be completed within three months of purchase.

Most stores in German-speaking countries are not open for as long as stores in the United States. Most stores will not be open on Sunday or after eight p.m or even earlier. Stores hours are regulated by law, and vary by region. In an emergency, try looking for stores in a train station, as these are usually open longer than other stores.

In Germany, the mail is carried by Deutsche Post, with its distinctive yellow and black signs. The symbol of the Deutsche Post is the round Posthorn that mail carriers used to carry. The Deutsche Post uses its international arm, DHL, to send packages all over the world. The German postal system is similar to the American system, and its post offices are general modern and easy to use. Postage can be purchased online or at computer kiosks in the post office.

When addressing a letter to a European address, remember that the zip code usually comes before the city, instead of the other way around.

In Switzerland, the mail is carried by Swiss Post, whose color is also yellow, with the symbol of a red cross instead of a post horn.

In Austria, the mail is carried by die Österreichische Post/the Austrian Post or just Post. Its symbol is a yellow post horn.

Vocabulary: Shopping

Nouns:

German	English
die Quittung	the receipt
das Bargeld	the cash
die Kreditkarte	the credit card
die Lastschrift	the debit transaction
die Münze	the coin
die Kasse	the cash register
der Beutel	the bag
die Lebensmittel	the groceries
das Kaufhaus	the department store
der Preis	the price
die Öffnungszeiten	the hours of operation
der Kassierer	the cashier
der Einkaufswagen	the shopping cart
das Portemonnaie	the wallet
die Steuer	the tax
das Angebot	the offer/deal

German	English
der Coupon	the coupon
der Ausverkauf	the sale
der Kundendienst	customer service
die Größe	the size

Verbs:

German	English
kaufen	to buy
verkaufen	to sell
suchen	to look for
vergleichen	to compare
kosten	to cost
verhandeln	to deal
sparen	to save (money)
bezahlen	to pay
zurückgeben	to return
einkaufen	to buy/ to shop
ersetzen	to exchange
sich umsehen	to browse
vergleichen	to compare

Phrases:

German	English
Das ist billig.	That is cheap.
Das ist teuer.	That is expensive.
Wie viel kostet es?	How much does it cost?
Wo findet man…	Where does one find…
Ich bezahle mit…	I am paying with…

Unit 3

Irregular Verbs

Irregular verbs don't play by the rules. Not only that, but there is really no warning when a verb will be irregular and what kind of rules it will follow. That is why it is important to memorize common irregular verbs so that you don't try to conjugate them like a regular verb.

Most irregular verbs still add endings like regular verbs. The difference comes in that they also change their vowel sounds with some subjects. This means, you don't need to throw everything you know about verbs out the window, but you do need to make sure you're playing by the correct set of rules.

One of the nice things about irregular verbs is that most of them are irregular in the same way. The same forms change their vowel sounds, so that they are easier to predict. Most irregular verbs change their vowel sounds in the "du" and the "er/sie/es" forms.

Here are some examples of irregular verbs and how they change their vowel sounds:

German	English
Wir fahren. Er fährt.	We are driving. He is driving.

Wir laufen. Er läuft.	We are running. He is running.
Wir lesen. Er liest.	We are reading. He is reading.
Wir essen. Er isst.	We are eating. He is eating.
Wir geben. Er gibt.	We are giving. He is giving.
Wir helfen. Er hilft.	We are helping. He is helping.
Wir nehmen. Er nimmt.	We are taking. He is taking.
Wir schlagen. Er schlägt.	We are hitting. They are hitting.
Wir sprechen. Er spricht.	We are speaking. He is speaking.
Wir treffen. Er trifft.	We are meeting. He is meeting.

Remember that all the irregular verbs above do not change their vowel sounds in another of the other forms.

Two Rebel Verbs

There are two common verbs that are more irregular than others. They do not follow set patterns and so you will need to memorize them so that you can use them when they come up.

The first of these is *sein* or to be. It takes the following forms:

German	English
Ich bin.	I am
Du bist.	You are. (informal)

Er/Sie/Es ist.	He/She/It is.
Wir sind.	We are.
Ihr seid.	You all are. (informal)
Sie sind.	They are.
Sie sind.	You are. (formal)

The second of these verbs is **haben** or to have. It takes the following forms:

German	English
Ich habe.	I have.
Du hast.	You have. (informal)
Er/Sie/Es hat.	He/She/It has.
Wir haben.	We have.
Ihr habt.	You all have.
Sie haben.	They have.
Sie haben.	You have. (formal)

These verbs are important because they are also used as helping verbs to form the most common form of the past tense. It is important that you know them forward and backwards before you learn the past tense.

Pronunciation: The Letter S

The letter S behaves in different ways depending on the letters around it. Most of the time, it sounds exactly like the English letter Z. When S is the last letter in a word, it does not sound like a Z, but instead like an English S. Here are some examples of words that have an S that sounds like this:

S at the Beginning

German	English
sieben	seventeen
sechzehn	sixteen
der Sand	the sand
der Sänger	the singer
die Säge	the saw
simsen	to text
der Sommer	the summer
der See	the lake

S in the Middle

German	English
unser	our
die Insel	the island

German	English
reisen	to travel
die Rosen	the roses
die Speisen	the food

S at the End:

German	English
der Reis	the rice
der Preis	the price
der Atlas	the atlas

When two instances of the letter S are right next to each other, they make the sound like the English letter S. Two S's can sometimes be replaced by a letter unique to German called the Esszett (ß). Though it looks a lot like the capital letter B, make sure you say this like an S. Here are some examples words with the double S.

Double S Words

German	English
heißen	to be called
die Straße	the street
die Gasse	the avenue

When S is found next to P at the beginning of a

word, it makes a sound like the English letters SHP. Here are some examples of words that contain this comination.

SP at the Beginning

German	English
spielen	to play
sprechen	to speak
der Spass	the fun
der Specht	the bacon
das Spiel	the game
spotten	to mock
die Speise	the food

Culture: Eating at a Home

Many people from German-speaking countries and gracious and generous entertainers. When you visit someone in their home, expect that they will offer you something to drink. Sometimes, this will be sparkling water, and sometimes they will offer you water with various fruit juices. Many people will mix the sparkling water and juices together.

Other times, hosts will offer a variety of teas. Black tea (schwarzer Tee) and green tea (grüner Tee) should be avoided. There are many kinds of tea such as fruit tea (Früchtetee) and peppermint tea (Pfefferminztee), which are perfectly acceptable. If in doubt, consult your mission leadership.

When you sit down to a meal, it is usually polite not to start eating right away. Once everyone is seated, the head of the household with say something such as "Guten Apetit!", which indicates that everyone should start eating.

When you see a small spoon placed at the top of the plate, you can count on dessert. Some people call it "der kleine Prophet" (the little prophet), because it foretells the coming dessert. Do not, however, count on your dessert being as sugary sweet as the ones you might be used to. German-speakers serve a variety of desserts from pies and puddings, to red berries and cream, to ice cream and apple strudel.

You will also notice that Germans use their utensils differently. When people from the United States and other places eat a meal, they hold their fork in their left hand and the knife in their right, cut their food and then switch. Their fork ends up in their right hand and then is put down. Americans sometimes cut all of their meat at one time before setting the knife down. Then, they pick up their fork with their right hand and resume eating the meal, which is a lot more complex than German-speakers make it.

Instead, Germans-speakers hold their knife in their right hand, fork in their left. They will cut their food one piece at a time and not switch their utensils. They keep their fork in the left hand and eat with it, even if they are right handed. They keep their knife in their right hand so there is no switching between the two. After cutting the meat with the knife and fork, they stab the meat with the fork, keeping the fork upside down in the left hand. Then, take the fork to your mouth, still upside-down. Once they are done with eating, they place the knife and fork side by side on the plate. It is a good idea to learn how to eat in this fashion so that you blend in with your hosts.

Vocabulary: Numbers and Shapes

Nouns:

German	English
eins	one
zwei	two
drei	three
vier	four
fünf	five
sechs	six
sieben	seven
acht	eight
neun	nine
zehn	ten
elf	eleven
zwölf	twelve
dreizehn	thirteen
vierzehn	fourteen
fünfzehn	fifteen
sechzehn	sixteen

siebzehn	seventeen
achtzehn	eighteen
neunzehn	nineteen
zwanzig	twenty
einundzwanzig	twenty-one
dreißig	thirty
vierzig	forty
fünfzig	fifty
sechzig	sixty
siebzig	seventy
achtzig	eighty
neunzig	ninety
hundert	one hundred
tausend	one thousand
Million	one million
Millarde	one billion
Billion	one trillion
Billiarde	one quadrillion
das Viereck	the square

der Kreis	the circle
das Dreieck	the triangle
das Rechteck	the rectangle
das Oval	the oval
das Achteck	the octagon
der Würfel	the cube
die Kugel	the sphere
der Kegel	the cone
der Zylinder	the cylinder
der Winkel	the angel
die Linie	the line
der Graph	the graph

Verbs:

German	English
zählen	to count
addieren	to add
subtrahieren	to subtract
multiplizieren	to multiply
dividieren	to divide

Phrases:

German	English
Wie viel ist...?	How much is...?
Ist gleich	is equal to
Eins plus eins ist...	One plus one is...
Sechs minus fünf ist...	Six minus five is...
Zehn mal zehn ist...	Ten times ten is...
Zehn durch zwei ist...	Ten divided by two is...

Unit 4

Grammar: Questions and Commands

Questions

There are two ways to form questions in German. The first is to reverse the subject and the verb in a statement.

German	English
Sie kennen die Missionare.	You know the missionaries.
Kennen Sie die Missionare?	Do you know the missionaries?
Du isst Wurst.	You are eating sausage.
Isst du Wurst?	Are you eating sausage?
Sie sprechen das Gebet.	You are saying the prayer.
Sprechen Sie das Gebet?	Are you saying the prayer?

The second way to form a question is to start the sentence with a question word. Like most question words in English, the German question words start with W.

German	English
wo	where
wer	who
was	what

wann	when
wie	how
warum	why
wie viel	how much
wie viele	how many

Be sure to pay attention to the difference between wie viel and wie viele. The difference is the same between how much and how many in English. You use how much/wie viel when talking about amounts such as cups, liters or gallons such as milk, water, or sugar. You would never, for example, say that you have a cup of cookies.

Use how many/wie viele when talking about things that can be numbered like cookies, cups or spoons.

Commands

All German commands are given an exclamation point at the end, but this does not necessarily mean they are shouted. When giving a command, you first need to consider your audience. There are three different kinds of commands, depending on to whom you are speaking. These are the du form (informal, singular), the ihr form (informal, plural) and the Sie form (formal, singular or plural).

The Sie form is the simplest form, and should be

used in any formal situation. You first say the infinitive form of the verb and then the word *Sie*. Take a look at a few examples of this.

German	English
Spielen Sie!	Play!
Essen Sie!	Eat!
Springen Sie!	Jump!
Laufen Sie!	Run!
Singen Sie!	Sing!
Beten Sie!	Pray!

The du form leaves off the word "you" altogether, and should be used when talking to one person informally. You first conjugate the verb to its du form (including the vowel change from irregular verbs) and then drop off the –st ending. Compare this form to the previous examples.

German	English
Spiel!	Play!
Iss!	Eat!
Spring!	Jump!
Lauf!	Run!

Sing!	Sing!
Bete!	Pray!

The *ihr* form also leaves off the word "you" and should be used when you are talking to more than one person informally. You simply use the *ihr* form of the verb in this case. This means that you do not change the vowel sounds for irregular verbs. See how this compares to the previous examples.

German	English
Spielt!	Play!
Esst!	Eat!
Springt!	Jump!
Lauft!	Run!
Singt!	Sing!
Betet!	Pray!

There is another form used for making suggestions that is straightforward. It uses *wir* as the subject and the verb keeps its infinitive form.

German	English
Spielen wir!	Let's play!
Essen wir!	Let's eat!

Springen wir!	Let's jump!
Laufen wir!	Let's run!
Singen wir!	Let's sing!
Beten wir!	Let's pray!

Pronunciation: The Letter W

The letter W can be a little tricky for English speakers. It always sounds like the English letter V. This is especially important to remember because it shows up so often in German words. The good thing is that it is consistent—no matter where you see it in a word, it will sound like an English V. The letter V in German, usually sounds like an English F, though in some words, it retains its V sound, such as in the word November.

Here are some words that demonstrate the letter W:

W at the Beginning:

German	English
die Wolke	the cloud
die Wand	the wall
die Wunde	the wound
das Wasser	the water
das Wunder	the miracle
die Welt	the world
wachsen	to grow
widmen	to dedicate
waschen	to wash

werden	to become

W in the Middle:

German	English
die Möwe	the seagull
der Gewinn	the profit
erwarten	to anticipate
zweifeln	to doubt
der Vorwurf	the accusation
unterwegs	underway

Culture: Eating at a Restaurant

When eating at a restaurant in a German-speaking country, there are several things that you might have to get used to. First, is that many restaurants seat multiple parties at a single table, even if they are strangers.

When ordering drinks, remember that if you order water, you will most likely receive carbonated water without any ice. It is rare that a restaurant serves free water. You can ask for **Leitungswasser** or tap water, which they may serve you. If you order any other drink, it will likely not be served with ice, and you will probably not be offered free refills. Most Europeans are not used to drinking cold drinks and so this is something that you should become accustomed to.

If you are looking for a restaurant that serves soft drinks with ice and offers free refills, you will probably need to visit an American fast-food chain such as McDonalds, Burger King, or Kentucky Fried Chicken.

It is still customary to leave a tip (**Trinkgeld**), though it is not expected to be as large as is usually in the United States. You often simply round up to the next full Euro amount or so.

There are a great variety of restaurants in German-speaking countries, especially Turkish restaurants and Asian restaurants. It is much rarer to find Mexican restaurants or restaurants that serve American-style pizza. The pizza you will likely find is closer to the Italian style pizza, which has a thin crust and a greater variety of toppings.

Ice cream parlors are popular in German-speaking countries, especially Italian ice cream, also known as gelato.

Vocabulary: Restaurant

Nouns:

German	English
German	**English**
das Restaurant	the restaurant
der Tisch	the table
der Kellner	the waiter (male)
die Kellnerin	the waitress
die Rechnung	the bill
das Trinkgeld	the tip (money)
die Speisekarte	the menu
der Stuhl	the chair
die Vorspeise	the appetizer
das Hauptgericht	the main course
das Nebengericht	the side dish
der Nachtisch	the dessert
das Getränk	the drink
das Wasser	the water
die Milch	the milk
das Frühstück	the breakfast

das Mittagesen	the lunch
das Abendessen	the dinner
der Imbiss	the snack
der Teller	the plate
das Messer	the knife
die Gabel	the fork
der Löffel	the spoon
das Glas	the glass
die Tasse	the cup
die Serviette	the napkin

Verbs:

German	English
essen	to eat
trinken	to drink
bestellen	to order
danken	to thank
kochen	to cook
vorbereiten	to prepare

schneiden	to cut
den Tisch decken	to set the table

Phrases:

German	**English**
Schmeckt es dir?	Does it taste good?
Es schmeckt.	It tastes good.
Das ist lecker!	That is tasty.
Guten Apetit!	Bon apetit/Enjoy your meal.
Lass es dir schmecken!	Enjoy your meal!

Unit 5

Grammar: Accusative Case

You've seen what it means to be in the nominative case. Nouns in this case act as the subjects of the sentence. Another case that you will need to know is the accusative case. The accusative case is used for the direct object or the receiver of the action in a sentence. It answers the question of what is being acted upon.

First, let's look at a few examples in English.

The boy sees the girl. (*The girl* is the direct object)

The dog bites the man. (*The man* is the direct object)

The woman eats the pizza. (*The pizza* is the direct object)

Now in German:

Der Junge sieht das Mädchen.

Der Hund beißt den Mann.

Die Frau isst die Pizza.

Did you notice the new article in the examples? Instead of saying Der Hund beißt der Mann, you have to say Der Hund beißt den Mann. The word der changes to den in the accusative case. Here are a few sentences that demonstrate this new pattern.

German	English
Das Mädchen sieht den Jungen.	The girl sees the boy.
Der Junge ruft den Hund.	The boy calls the dog.
Die Frau kocht das Ei.	The woman cooks the egg.

The other articles do not change in the accusative case. Die stays die and das stays das. For this reason, you need to make sure you know what case a noun is in and focus on the nominative ones. Notice this in the following examples:

German	English
Der Mann sieht die Frau.	The man sees the woman.
Die Frau sieht das Kind.	The woman sees the child.
Der Mann ruft das Kind.	The man calls the child.
Das Kind ruft die Frau.	The child calls the woman.

There are some prepositions that automatically make the nouns after them accusative. They are as follows:

German	English
durch	through
für	for
gegen	against

ohne	without
um	around
entlang	along

Usually, these prepositions come before the nouns they modify, but often, you will hear the word *entlang* after the noun it modifies. Remember that you still need to change the article if it is a masculine word.

German	English
Ich laufe den Fluss entlang.	I am running along the river.
Wir fahren die Strasse entlang.	We drive along the street.

Pronunciation: The Letter V

The letter V can be tricky for English speakers, because it doesn't often sound like the V you know and love. Instead, most of the time if sounds like and English F. no matter where it is in the word, though there are some borrowed words in which it sounds like it does in English. Here are a few examples:

V at the Beginning

German	English
vier	four
das Volk	the people
der Vorschlag	the suggestion
die Verpflichtung	the commitment
verkaufen	to sell

V at the End

German	English
brav	well-behaved
das Leitmotiv	the leading motif (music)

There are some words, especially those shared with other languages, in which the V sounds like an English V. Here are a few examples of words like this:

German	English
die Vase	the vase
November	November

Culture: Public Transportation

If you like public transportation, than you are in luck. In German-speaking countries, you can usually get anywhere you want to go quickly using public transportation. Especially if you live in a big city, regular buses, trains, subways, and streetcars are never far away.

At most bus stops and train stations, you will see a machine where you can buy tickets. There are a variety of passes that you can buy, and you should consider how much you will be traveling to see what would be most cost-effective. For example, you can buy daily, monthly, or even yearly passes that allow you unlimited travel. Sometimes, the mission office will reimburse missionaries for such passes. Check with the mission office to find out what the policy in your mission is.

A network of high-speed trains also runs through many European countries. These trains are called IC (for Inter-City) or ICE (Inter-City Express) and can travel rapidly between cities. They are, however, much more expensive than regular train travel, and so it is not as likely that you will ride them as a missionary.

Tickets will not be checked on every train ride, but are checked periodiacally by transportation employees. A person in uniform, known as a

Schaffner, will make his or her way through the train and ask to see everyone's tickets. If you cannot produce a ticket, you are a Schwarzfahrer (literally "black rider") and will be forced to pay a hefty fine. Never risk riding a train without a ticket.

Vocabulary: Public Transportation

Nouns:

German	English
der Zug	the train
der Bahnhof	the train station
die U-bahn	the subway
die Strassenbahn	the streetcar
die Fahrkarte	the ticket (transportation)
der Bus	the bus
die Bushaltestelle	the bus station
der Schaffner	the conductor
der Fahrer	the driver
der Sitzplatz	the seat

Verbs:

German	English
fahren	to drive
einsteigen	to embark
aussteigen	to disembark

sich hinsetzen   to sit down

aufstehen   to stand up

Phrases:

German	English
Einfach oder hin und zurück?	One-way or round trip?
Wann kommt der Bus?	When is the bus coming?
Ist der Zug verspätet?	Is the train delayed?
Fahrkarte, bitte.	Tickets, please.
Wann fährt der Bus ab?	When does the bus leave?

Unit 6

Grammar: Adjectives

In both German and English, adjectives are words that describe nouns. Adjectives are words like big, blue, beautiful, faithful, expensive or tall.

It is much simpler to use adjectives in English than in German. You place them in front of a noun as is and never have to change them. In German, however, using adjectives can be a complex process. Adjectives still usually appear before the nouns they modify, but often take different endings, depending on several factors including the number, case, and gender of the noun they modify.

Much depends on whether or not a definite or indefinite article is present. One good thing to remember, is that between the articles and adjectives, something will take an ending that will show the case and gender of the noun.

First, let's talk about adjectives with definite articles. If a definite article is present, adjectives take the following endings: either –e or –en.

	Masculine	Feminine	Neuter
Nom	der alte Hund	die nette Lehrerin	das heiße Essen
Acc	den alten Hund	die nette Lehrerin	das heiße Essen
Dat.	dem alten Hund	der netten Lehrerin	dem heißen Essen
Gen.	des alten Hundes	der netten Lehrerin	des heißen Essens

Plural words, which always take the article die, always cause the adjectives after them to add –en.

	Plural
Nominative	die schwarzen Kulis
Accusative	die schwarzen Kulis
Dative	den schwarzen Kulis
Genitive	der schwarzen Kulis

Another way to think of this, is to add –e when the article does not change from its usual der, die, or das form. Add –en if the article changes to something else like dem, den, or der, or is a plural word.

Now, let's talk about adjectives with indefinite articles. If an indefinite article is present, the endings are a little different. Notice that endings can be –er, -e, -es, -en. Because indefinite articles describe singular things, there is no need to discuss plural forms with indefinite articles.

	Masculine	Feminine	Neuter
Nom.	ein großer Hund	eine nette Lehrerin	ein heißes Essen
Acc.	einen großen Hund	eine nette Lehrerin	ein heißes Essen
Dat.	einem großen Hund	einer großen Lehrerin	einem großen Essen
Gen.	eines großen Hund(es)	einer großen Lehrerin	eines großen Essen

Notice that you have to show the difference between masculine and neuter in the nominative case by adding either *er* or *es*. Otherwise, you would not be able to tell them apart. Learning adjectives can take some practice, but don't be discouraged. It is something you will get an ear for over time.

Pronunciation: The Letter Q

The letter Q is one of those, which can cause trouble for English speakers. Instead of producing the sound of an English Q such as in the word queen, it produced a sound like the combination of English letters KV.

Similar to English, you almost always see it with U as it companion. Here are some examples of words that demonstrate the letter Q.

Q at the Beginning

German	English
die Qualle	the jellyfish
die Quittung	the receipt
die Quelle	the source
der Quatsch	the nonsense
der Quadratmeter	the square meter
quietschen	to squeak
quer	diagonally

Culture: Driving

Though some of the fanciest cars in the world come from Germany, many people do not rely on cars as their primary means of transportation. The public transportation system in Germany, Austria, and Switzerland is much more developed than in the United States, especially in large cities. You can take trains, buses, streetcars and subways just about anywhere you want to go.

Also contributing to the reason some people forgo a car is the high price of gasoline. When you drive by a gas station, you might think the prices look low, but you have to remember that the price is per liter and not per gallon. There are approximately 3.2 liters in every gallon, so you have to take that price and multiply it by 3.2 and then convert it into Euro. The Euro is generally stronger than the dollar, making the cost even higher. This means that driving is simply not affordable for many German speakers.

Because they want to get the most out of their fuel, German speakers tend to drive cars with manual transmissions. A vast majority of the cars you will see will not have automatic transmissions, and so chances are that if you are given a car in your area, you'll have to learn to drive a stick shift.

The German word for freeway is **Autobahn**. There

is a common misconception that that the Autobahn has no speed limit. While there are sections of the Autobahn that have no speed limit, there are many sections that do.

Speed limit signs are round signs with a ring of red around the edge and a number in the middle. This number in black digits is the speed limit in kilometers per hour. Remember that each kilometer per hour is not as much as a mile per hour. The highest posted speed limit you will see is 130 km/hr, which is about 80 m/hr. You will also see a round white sign with diagonal black lines through the center. This means **unbegrenzt** (unlimited), which means that there is no speed limit.

Be sure to consult your mission leadership at to what the maximum speed limit for missionaries is. Chances are, you will not be able to drive as fast as you want or can in order to keep you and your companion safe. In sections of the Autobahn where there is no speed limit, it is probably a good idea not to drive in the fast lane, because many German drivers with powerful cars will be testing the limits of their machines, and will not be too happy if you are in their way.

You will notice that stop signs look the same in Germany, but most other streets signs will not. Any round sign with a red ring around the edge means that whatever is inside the circle is forbidden.

If you see a sign that has three diagonal black lines or one thick red line through it, this sign is cancelling out a pervious sign of the same type. This can cancel a speed limit or another other kind of sign.

Triangular signs generally provide some sort of warning, such as an approaching traffic light, a railway crossing, or rough road ahead.

Stop Signs = these look exactly like they do in the United States.

Priority road = there are signs with a yellow diamond inside a white diamond. This means that you have the right of way until you see another sign ending it. You may not park on these roads.

Yield Sign = this is an upside-down white triangle with a red rim. It does not have any text on it.

No Passing = this is a white circle with a red rim in which there are two cars, one red and one black.

Do Not Enter = this is a blank white circle with a red rim or a red circle with a white line through the center

One-Way Street = this is a rectangular sign with an arrow pointing in one direction. The word "Einbahnstraße" is printed in the arrow.

Pedestrian Zone = this is a round blue sign with a white mother and child on it

Autobahn Entrance = this is blue square with a white road with an overpass on it

No Parking = this is a blue circle with a red rim and a red X through it.

City Signs = these are yellow rectangular signs that show you what city you are entering. Sometimes they will be split in half with a red line through one city name. This means you are leaving one city and enter another.

Exit = This an arrow-shaped sign with the word "Ausfahrt" written on it.

Detour = these are yellow signs that might be arrow-shaped that have word "Umleitung" on them.

Dead End = this sign is a blue square sign with a red and white line forming a T in the center.

Traffic lights also act slightly differently. In the United States, traffic lights turn yellow before they turn red. In German-speaking countries, the light also turns yellow right before it turns green again, allowing motorist to prepare to move.

In German-speaking countries you will need to be aware of traffic cameras. Some of these cameras are mounted in permanent locations, while some of them are set up temporarily. These cameras have sensors that automatically detect if a car is speeding or runs a red light. The camera automatically takes a picture that captures the image of license plate and who is driving the car. You will then receive a citation in the mail that you will be expected to pay. There is no telling where these cameras might be, so it is best not to risk speeding, even if you are late to an appointment.

Obtaining a Driver's License

Driver's licenses from other countries are not valid in German-speaking countries. However, once you obtained a driver's license it is valid for the rest of your life and for the entire European Union. (Note that this does not include Switzerland)

Obtaining a driver's license is more difficult for people in German-speaking countries. They must be 18 before obtaining one, and they must attend an expensive **Fahrschule** (driving school). If you have a driver's license from a U.S. state, you might be able to convert it to a German license by surrendering your old license and paying a small fee. Some U.S. states might require you to take a written test or other additional requirements. Check with your local TÜV (DMV) to figure out the requirements.

Vocabulary: In the Car

Nouns:

German	English
das Auto	the car
der Wagen	the car
der Lastwagen	the truck
die Bremsen	the brakes
das Lenkrad	the steering wheel
das Rad	the wheel
die Reifen	the tires
die Windschutzscheibe	the windshield
der Sitzplatz	the seat
die Autotür	the car door
das Benzin	the gasoline
die Tankstelle	the gas station
der Motor	the motor
die Ampel	the traffic light
das Stopschild	the stop sign
die Spur	the lane

die Geschwindigkeitsbegrenzung   the speed limit

die Autobahn   the freeway

die Landstraße   the highway

die Straße   the street

die Klimaanlage   the air conditioning

der CD Spieler   the CD player

der Rückspiegel   the rearview mirror

der Kofferraum   the trunk

der Benzintank   the gas tank

die Antenne   the antenna

der Sicherheitsgurt   the seat belt

das Bremslicht   the brake light

der Scheibenwischer   the windshield wipers

die Adresse   the address

die Landkarte   the map

die Ecke   the corner

die Kreuzung   the intersection

der Stau   the traffic

der Polizeiwagen   the police car

German	English
der Strafzettel	the ticket (punishment)
die Tankstelle	the gas station
Nord	north
Süd	south
Ost	east
West	west
dort	there
hier	here
rechts	right
links	left
nah	near
weit	far
geradeaus	straight

Verbs:

German	English
fahren	to drive
abbiegen	to turn
bremsen	to brake

anhalten	to stop
steuern	to steer
halten	to stop
lenken	to steer
überqueren	to cross
laufen	to run
entlang gehen	to go along
sich beschleunigen	to accelerate
einen Unfall haben	to have an accident
parken	to park

Phrases:

German	**English**
das Auto waschen	to wash the car
einen Autounfall haben	to have a car accident
zu schnell fahren	to drive too fast
Wie komme ich zu ___?	How do I get to _____?
Ist es weit?	Is it far?
Biegen Sie hier links/rechts.	Turn right/left here.
Fahre immer geradeaus.	Keep driving straight.

Das ist nördlich von hier.   That is north of here.

Unit 7

Grammar: Conjunctions

In German, just like in English, there are two kinds of conjunctions: coordinating and subordinating conjunctions. Conjunctions connect nouns, phrases, clauses or sentences. In German, coordinating conjunctions do not change the word order of the sentence, while subordinating conjunctions do.

Coordinating conjunctions in German include:

German	English
und	and
aber	but
oder	or
denn	because
sondern	but rather

Here are a few example sentences. Notice that these do not affect word order.

German	English
Wir benutzen den Bus **und** den Zug.	We use the bus and the train.
Er will beten **aber** weiß nicht wie.	He wants to pray but does know how.
Kaufen wir bei Aldi **oder** Netto ein?	Are we shopping at Aldi or Netto?
Sie kommt nicht, **denn** sie ist krank.	She is not coming, because she's sick.

Ich trinke keinen Tee **sondern** Wasser.   I am not drinking tea, but rather water.

Subordinating conjunctions in German include:

German	English
weil	because
als	as, when
wenn	if, whenever
damit	so that
ob	if, whether
dass	that
nachdem	after

Here are a few example sentences. Notice that these are always set off by a comma and send the verb to the end of the sentence of clause that they are in. This is very important in order to sound like a competent German speaker.

German	English
Er glaubt, **weil** er gebetet hat.	He believes, because he prayed.
Als er jung war, ging er in die Kirche.	When he was young, he went to church.
Wenn man dient, fühlt man sich gut.	Whenever you serve, you feel good.
Wir schlafen, **damit** wir besser werden.	We sleep so that we'll get better.
Wissen Sie, **ob** es einen Gott gibt?	Do you know if there is a God?

Ich weiß, **dass** es einen Gott gibt.	I know that there is a God.
Nachdem wir essen, lernen wir.	After we eat, we study.

In addition to the common conjunctions above, all interrogative words (wann, wie, wer, warum, etc) can be used as subordinating conjunctions.

German

English

German	English
Wissen Sie, wann er ankommt?	Do you know when he's arriving?
Wissen Sie, wo die Kirche ist?	Do you know where the church is?
Wissen Sie, wer der Prophet ist?	Do you know who the prophet is?
Wissen Sie, was wir glauben?	Do you know what we believe?
Wissen Sie, warum wir hier sind?	Do you know why we are here?
Wissen Sie, wie er heißt?	Do you know how he's called?
Wissen Sie wie viel es kostet?	Do you know how much it costs?

Pronunciation: The Letter R

The letter R in German can be tricky, and getting it right is essential to having a good German accent. The most important thing to remember is to never pronounce an R in German like your do in English.

One option for pronouncing R, is rolling the R on the front of your tongue like you might have heard Spanish speakers do. You do not, however, roll it nearly as long as a Spanish R trill—just a short flip. The only time you will hear long rolled Rs is on stage, such as in an opera.

The best way to pronounce R is to roll it briefly in the back of your throat in a sensation like that of gargling water. This can take some practice, but will help you sound more authentic. Remember, there is only one wrong way to pronounce R—the American way.

The only time that R is pronounced differently is when it shows up as –er. In this case, it sounds similar to a final –e. This combination is usually seen at the end of words such as Vater and Mutter, and in prefixes such as *ver-*, *zer-*, and *her*.

Here are some examples of words that incorporate the letter R.

R and the Beginning

German	English
der Regen	the rain
die Reise	the trip
der Rock	the skirt
der Riese	the giant
der Ritter	the knight
das Rechteck	the rectangle
der Regenbogen	the rainbow
recht	right
richtig	correct
regelmässig	regularly
rot	red

R in the Middle

German	English
verzeihen	to forgive
herstellen	to manufacture
verstecken	to hide

versprechen	to promise
zerstören	to destroy
der Frieden	the peace
die Strafe	the punishment
die Kreide	the chalk
Frankreich	France

R at the End

German	English
der Vater	the father
die Mutter	the mother
der Bruder	the brother
die Schwester	the sister

Culture: Holidays

German-speaking countries celebrate many of the same holidays that the United States does. Such holidays, include Easter, Christmas, Mother's Day and Father's Day. Sometimes, however, these shared holidays are celebrated on different days than in the United States.

There are also many holidays, especially religious holidays that are still celebrated in Germany. Though many Germans receive the day off of work for these days, many Germans do not understand the religious significance of the day.

Shared Holidays

German-speaking countries celebrate Christmas and it is known as Weihnachten. They enjoy this season so much that they celebrate it over three days: December 24th (called Heiligabend), December 25th (1st Christmas Day/Erster Weihnachtsfeiertag) and December 26th (2nd Christmas Day/Zweiter Weihnachtsfeiertag). On Christmas Eve, many families sing Stille Nacht (Silent Night), and receive presents from each other. Presents are not brought by Santa Claus, though he does make an appearance in the month of December.

Mother's Day and Father's Day are both

celebrated, but on different days than their American counterparts. Easter is also celebrated and falls on the same day as in the United States. They do not, however, usually celebrate with colored eggs and the Easter Bunny.

German-speaking countries celebrate Thanksgiving or Erntedankfest, but do so in October instead of November. Families and friends typically gather for a large meal.

Most German-speakers do not celebrate Halloween, but there is a growing trend of those adopting this American holiday.

Unique Holidays

Tag der Deutschen Einheit (Day of German Unity) is the German national holiday, which is comparable to Independence Day in the United States. It is celebrated on October 3rd, because this was the day that East Germany and West Germany were united into one country again.

Saint Nicholas Day (Sankt Nicholas Tag) is December 6th. On the night before, the children in the household lay out their shoes in a row and in the morning, they find them filled with candy and presents.

Holy Three Kings Day (Dreikönigstag) is celebrated

on January 6th as the traditional date on which the Wise Men visited Jesus as a child. On this day, groups of children dress up in robes and turbans like the Wise Men and carry staffs with a star on top. They walk from house to house, singing and having a good time. They visit each house and collect money for the poor. At each house, they write C + M + B and on the top of the doorframe in chalk. These letters stand for the Latin phrase that means "Christ bless this house", and also stand for the traditional names of the Wise Men: Caspar, Melchior, and Balthazar.

In some Catholic regions, November 1st is an official holiday called Allerheiligen (All Saints Day). On this day, worshipers go to church to honor the Saints and meet together to eat and celebrate. The day after is known as Allersellen, or All Souls Day, in which the spirits of the dead are said to walk the earth. People honor those relatives who have passed on and visit their graves.

There are a variety of minor religious holidays that are celebrated according to the predominant religion of the region. Here is a chart of some of the holidays in various German-speaking regions:

HOLIDAYS with FIXED DATES		
January-June | Januar-Juni		
Feiertag	Holiday	Datum/Date
JANUAR		
Neujahr*	New Year's Day	1. Januar (am ersten Januar)
Heilige Drei Könige*	Epiphany, Three Kings	6. Januar (am sechsten Januar) A public holiday in Austria and the states of Baden-Württemberg, Bayern (Bavaria), and Sachsen-Anhalt in Germany.
FEBRUAR		
Mariä Lichtmess	Candlemas (Groundhog Day)	2. Februar (am zweiten Feb.) Catholic regions
Valentinstag	Valentine's Day	14. Februar (am vierzehnten Feb.)
Fasching, Karneval	Mardi Gras Carnival	In Catholic regions in Feb. or Mar., depending on the date of Easter. See Movable Feasts
MÄRZ		
Tag der Kranken	Day of the Ill	am ersten Sonntag im März (first Sunday in March; only in Switzerland)
Internationaler Frauentag	International Women's Day	8. März (am achten März)
Josephstag	St. Joseph's Day	19. März (am neunzehnten März; only in parts of Switzerland)
Mariä Verkündigung	Annunciation	25. März (am fünfundzwanzigsten März)
APRIL		
Erster April	April Fool's Day	1. April (am ersten April)
Karfreitag*	Good Day	Friday before Easter;
Ostern	Easter	Ostern falls in March or April,

		depending on the year; seeMovable Feasts
Walpurgisnacht	Walpurgis Night	30. April (am dreißigsten April) in Germany (Harz). Witches (Hexen) gather on eve of St. Walpurga's feast day (May Day).
MAI		
Erster Mai* Tag der Arbeit	May Day Labor Day	1. Mai (am ersten Mai)
Muttertag	Mother's Day	2nd Sunday in May (Austria, Germany, Switz.)
National holiday		
JUNI		
Vatertag	Father's Day	12. Juni 2005 2nd Sunday in June (Austria only; diff. date in Germany)
Johannistag	St. John the Baptist's Day	24. Juni (am vierundzwanzigsten Juni)
Siebenschläfer	St. Swithin's Day	27. Juni (am siebenundzwanzigsten Juni) Folklore: If it rains on this day it will rain for the next seven weeks. A Siebenschläfer is a dormouse.
Feiertag	Holiday	Datum/Date
JULI		
Gedenktag des Attentats auf Hitler 1944**	Commemorative day of the assassination attempt on Hitler in 1944	20. Juli - Germany

**This is more of an observance than an official holiday. On July 20, 1944 an assassination plot against Hitler failed when a bomb placed by Claus Schenk Graf von Stauffenberg detonated but only injured the dictator slightly. Von Stauffenberg and his fellow conspirators were arrested and hanged. Today von Stauffenberg and the other plotters are recognized for trying to end Nazi terror and restore democracy in Germany.

AUGUST		
National-feiertag*	Swiss National Day	1. August (am ersten Aug.) Celebrated with fireworks
Mariä Himmelfahrt	Assumption	15. August
SEPTEMBER		
Michaelis (das) der Michaelistag	Michaelmas (Feast of St. Michael the Archangel)	29. September (am neunundzwangzigsten Sept.)
Oktoberfest München	Oktoberfest - Munich	Two-week celebration beginning in late Sept. and ending on the first Sunday in October.
Erntedankfest	German Thanksgiving	End of September or early October; not an official holiday
OKTOBER		
Tag der deutschen Einheit*	Day of German Unity	3. Oktober - Germany's national holiday was moved to this date after the Berlin Wall came down.
National-feiertag*	National Holiday (Austria)	26. Oktober (am sechsundzwanzigsten Okt.) Austria's national holiday, called Flag Day, commemorates the founding of the Republik Österreich in 1955.
Halloween	Halloween	31. Oktober (am einunddreißigsten Okt.) Halloween is not a traditional German celebration, but in recent years it has become increasingly popular in

		Austria and Germany.
	NOVEMBER	
Allerheiligen	All Saints' Day	1. November (am ersten Nov.)
Allerseelen	All Souls' Day	2. November (am zweiten Nov.)
For the Protestant version of the Catholic All Soul's Day, see Movable Holidays and Totensonntag in November.		
Martinstag	Martinmas	11. November (am elften Nov.) Traditional roast goose (Martinsgans) and lantern light processsions for children on the evening of the 10th. The 11th is also the official start of theFasching/Karneval season in some regions.
	DEZEMBER	
Nikolaustag	St. Nicholas Day	6. Dezember (am sechsten Dez.) - On this day the white-bearded St. Nicholas (not Santa Claus) brings gifts to children who left their shoes in front of the door the night before.
Mariä Empfängnis	Feast of the Immaculate Conception	8. Dezember (am achten Dez.)
Heiligabend	Christmas Eve	24. Dezember (am vierundzwanzigsten Dez.) - This is when German children receive their presents (die Bescherung) around the Christmas tree (der Tannenbaum).
For Christmas and New Year's vocabulary see our English-German Christmas Glossary and Silvester Glossary.		
Weihnachten*	Christmas Day	25. Dezember (am fünfundzwanzigsten Dez.).

Zweiter Weihnachttsfeiertag*	Second Day of Christmas	26. Dezember (am sechsundzwanzigsten Dez.). Known as Stephanstag, St. Stephen's Day, in Austria.
Silvester	New Year's Eve	31. Dezember (am einunddreißigsten Dez.).

See:
http://german.about.com/library/blfkalender.htm

There are other holidays that do not have a fixed date, but fall on certain times of the year. Here is a list of some of these for German-speaking regions:

Movable Feasts | Bewegliche Feste		
Feiertag	Holiday	Datum/Date
JANUAR - FEBRUAR - MÄRZ		
Schmutziger Donnerstag Weiberfastnacht	Dirty Thursday Women's Carnival	Last Thursday of Fasching/Karneval when women traditionally snip off men's ties
Rosenmontag	Rose Monday	Date depends on Easter (Ostern) - Date of Karneval parades in the Rheinland - 4 Feb. 2008, 23 Feb. 2009
Fastnacht Karneval	Shrove Tuesday "Mardi Gras"	Date depends on Easter (Ostern) - Carnival (Mardi Gras)
Fasching / Shrove Tuesday: 5 Feb. 2008, 24 Feb. 2009		
Aschermittwoch	Ash Wednesday	End of the Carnival season; start of Lent (Fastenzeit)
Aschermittwoch / Ash Wednesday: 6 Feb. 2008, 25 Feb. 2009		
APRIL - MAI - JUNI		
Also see Name Days in April		

Palmsonntag	Palmsunday	Sunday before Easter (Ostern)
Beginn des Passahfestes	First Day of Passover	
Gründonnerstag	Maundy Thursday	Thursday before Easter From Latin mandatum in the prayer for Christ's washing of the feet of the disciples on the Thursday before Easter.
Karfreitag	Good Friday	Friday before Easter
Ostern Ostersonntag*	Easter Easter Sunday	On the first Sunday following the first full moon of spring
Ostern / Easter: 23 Mar. 2008, 12 Apr. 2009		
Ostermontag*	Easter Monday	A public holiday in Germany and most of Europe
Weißer Sonntag	Low Sunday	First Sunday after Easter Date of first communion in the Catholic church
Muttertag	Mother's Day	Second Sunday in May**
Muttertag / Mother's Day: 4 May 2008**		
**In Germany, if Mother's Day happens to fall on Pfingstsonntag (Pentecost), the date changes to the first Sunday in May.		
Christi Himmelfahrt	Ascension Day (of Jesus to heaven)	A public holiday; 40 days after Easter (see Vatertag below)
Vatertag	Father's Day	On Ascension Day in Germany. Not the same as the U.S. family-oriented Father's Day. In Austria it's in June.Learn more...
Pfingsten	Pentecost, Whitsun, Whit Sunday	A public holiday; the 7th Sun. after Easter. In some German statesPfingsten is a 2-week school holiday.
Pfingstmontag	Whit Monday	A public holiday

Pfingsten / Pentecost: 11 May 2008, 31 May 2009		
Fronleichnam	Corpus Christi	A public holiday in Austria and Catholic parts of Germany, Switzerland; Thursday following Trinity Sunday (the Sunday after Pentecost)
OCTOBER - NOVEMBER - DEZEMBER		
Volkstrauertag	National Day of Mourning	In November on the Sunday two weeks prior to the first Advent Sunday. In memory of Nazi victims and the dead in both world wars. Similar to Veteran's Day or Memorial Day in the US.
Buß- und Bettag	Day of Prayer and Repentance	The Wed. eleven days prior to the first Advent Sunday. A holiday in some regions only.
Totensonntag	Mourning Sunday	Observed in November on the Sunday prior to the first Advent Sunday. The Protestant version of All Soul's Day.
Erster Advent	First Sunday of Advent	The four-week Advent period leading up to Christmas is an important part of the German celebration.

See:

http://german.about.com/library/blfkalender.htm

Vocabulary: At Church

Nouns:

German	English
das Mitglied	the member
die Kirche	the church
der Bischof	the bishop
die Bischofschaft	the bishopric
der Berater	the counselor
die Kirchenbank	the pew
das Mikrofon	the microphone
das Abendmahl	the Sacrament
die Ansprache	the talk
das Lied	the song
das Gesangbuch	the hymnbook
das Gebet	the prayer
die Schriften	the scriptures
die Schriftstelle	the scripture passage
die Konferenz	the conference
das Kollegium	the quorum
die Klasse	the class
der Gemeindemissionsleiter	the ward mission leader
die Primarvereinigung	the primary
die Frauenhilfsvereinigung	the Relief Society
das Priestertum	the priesthood

Junge Männer	Young Men
Junge Damen	Young Women
der Chor	the choir
der Zweig	the branch
die Gemeinde	the ward
der Pfahl	the stake
der Prophet	the prophet
der Apostel	the apostle
der Tempel	the temple
das Anfangsgebet	the invocation
das Schlussgebet	the benediction

Verbs:

German	**English**
beten	to pray
grüßen	to greet
danken	to thank
lesen	to read
belehren	to teach
antworten	to answer
preisen	to praise

singen	to sing
Zeugnis geben	to bear testimony
essen	to eat
trinken	to drink
glauben	to believe
Orgel spielen	to play the organ
Klavier spielen	to play the piano
eine Ansprache geben	to give a talk
bekanntmachen	to announce
segnen	to bless
dienen	to serve
salben	to anoint
bestätigen	to confirm
taufen	to baptize
nachschlagen	to look up
vorlesen	to read aloud
anschauen	to look at

Phrases:

German	**English**
Liebe Brüder und Schwester	Dear brothers and sisters…

Ich weiß, dass…   I know that…

Unit 8

Grammar: Dative Case

The dative case is another way to use nouns in a sentence, like the nominative case used for subjects and the accusative case used for direct objects. The dative case is used for the indirect object.

This indirect object is the recipient of the direct object. It answers the question to whom or for whom? To whom did the subject give the direct object? Here are a few sentences to show you what this look likes.

English

I give the man the card.   "Man" is the indirect object.

The missionary gives me the book. "Me" is the indirect object.

German

Ich gebe dem Mann die Karte.   "dem Mann" instead of "der"

Der Missionar gibt mir das Buch.   "mir" instead of "mich"

The articles in the dative case change just like you saw in the accusative case. There are, however, more changes to learn with the dative case. The following chart shows the changes that happen.

In the case of a plural noun, you have to add the letter n to the plural form of the noun if there isn't already an n there. For example, the nominative for of *the child* is **das Kind**. The plural is **die Kinder**. The dative plural form is **den Kindern**, which means *to the children*.

Masculine	Feminine	Neuter	Plural
der to dem	die to der	das to dem	die to den (+n)
ein to einem	eine to einer	ein to einem	keine to keinen (+n)

Take a look at the following sentences. The nouns that are in the nominative case (acting as subjects) are writing in bold. The nouns that are in the accusative case (acting as direct objects) are italicized. The nouns that are in the dative case (acting as indirect objects) are underlined.

German	English
Ich werfe <u>der Frau</u> *das Brötchen zu.*	I am throwing the woman the roll.
Er sagt <u>dem Vater</u> *die Wahrheit.*	He is telling the father the truth.
Wir geben <u>dem Kind</u> *Geschenke.*	We are giving the child presents
Sie geben <u>den Kindern</u> *Schokolade*	They give the children chocolate.

You now know three different cases out of the four that German has and sometimes it can be difficult to keep them straight. To help you review, study the following chart that shows the forms all the articles take in all the cases that you have learned. If you are ever asking yourself what case something is in, just ask yourself what role or function the noun is playing in the sentence.

Mastering this list will go a long way toward making you sound like a natural German speaker.

	Masculine	Feminine	Neuter	Plural
Nom	der	die	das	die
Acc	den	die	das	die
Dat	dem	der	dem	den (+n)

As with the other cases, there are also certain prepositions that turn the nouns after them dative. You will learn more about these prepositions in a later lesson, but so that you can look out for them, here is a list of the most common dative prepositions.

German	English
aus	out
außer	except
bei	by, with
mit	with
nach	after, to
seit	since
von	from
zu	to

Pronunciation: The Letter J

You have to be careful with the letter J in German. It never makes the same sound that you hear in English, but instead the sound of the English letter Y. There are many German names, such as Johann, Jan, and Jens that start with the letter J, so it is especially important to pronounce it correctly.

Here are a few examples of German words that include the letter J.

German	English
der Jäger	the hunter
der Januar	January
der Juli	July
der Juni	June
das Jubiläum	the anniversary
der Joghurt	the yogurt
das Jahr	the year
die Jahreszeit	the season
japanisch	Japanese
das Jahrhundert	the century
das Jahrtausend	the millennium

jetzt	now
der Jude	the Jew
jung	young
der Juwelier	the jeweler
die Jugend	the youth

Culture: Religion

In German-speaking countries, there are two major religions: Catholic (die Katholische Kirche) and Protestant (die Evangelische Kirche). While you will run into people from all other world religions, these are the two that are most prevalent and recognized by the state.

Many people who live in German-speaking countries originally came from Turkey, and thus follow Islam. This will be vital to remember, as many of these people will not have a basic knowledge of Christianity that many natives will. There are also a significant number of Buddhists and Jews.

The Jehovah's Witnesses also have a strong presence in German-speaking countries. This is important to remember, because many people will mistake you for them, because they also have a prevalent missionary effort. You might even encounter their missionaries and if you do, you should be careful to avoid arguing with or confronting them.

Another common misconception about LDS missionaries is confusing them with Mennonites, which is a religion similar to the Amish. Most German speakers refer to members of the LDS Church as "Mormonen" and Mennonites as "Mennoniten", which in itself can cause some confusion. Mennonites do not drive cars or use electricity, among other differences, so you might have to explain the difference to people you meet on the street.

Originally, the Germanic tribes that occupied what are now the German-speaking countries of Europe worshiped a series of pagan gods such as Freyr, Baldr, and Wotan. These tribes were eventually taken over by the Roman Empire and Christianized. The Catholic Church was the dominant religion in the region for many years.

This changed with the advent of men such as Martin Luther, Huldrych Zwingli, John Calvin and others. Martin Luther disagreed with many of the practices of the Catholic Church. He sought only to reform the church, not to start a new one. He drafted 95 theses, or arguments against such Catholic Church, such as the selling of indulgences, the practice of being forgiven of sins for money.

The Catholic Church reacted strongly and excommunicated Luther and declared him a heretic. The spark of rebellion, however, had already been lit. Across Europe, religious-based conflicts flared and Europe descended into a bitter struggle known as the 30-Years War, in which Protestants and Catholics fought each other for supremacy.

At the end of the war, the lands split into smaller

kingdoms, each declaring allegiance to either the Protestant or the Catholic Church. Even though Germany and other German-speaking countries have merged these tiny kingdoms, some regions or states remained predominantly Catholic or Protestant to this day. This makes a difference especially when it comes to religious holidays, as some regions celebrate Catholic-only holidays, while others celebrate Protestant-only holidays.

Sometimes, you will hear churches refered to as "eine Sekte" or sect. This is a loose term that is often used for a church that does not fall within the realm of either Catholcism or Protestantism. It usually has a negative connotation, so it should be avoided and not applied to the Church of Jesus Christ of Latter-day Saints.

Vocabulary: Sight-Seeing and Holidays

Nouns:

German	English
German	**English**
der Urlaub	the vacation
der Feiertag	the holiday
der Vorbereitungstag	the preparation day
die Burg	the castle
das Schloss	the castle
die Festung	the fortress
der Dom	the cathedral
das Museum	the museum
das Hotel	the hotel
die Sehenswürdigkeit	the sight
die Landkarte	the map
die Broschüre	the brochure
die Eintrittskarten	the admission tickets
der Reiseführer	the tour guide
das Andenken	the souvenir
der Vergnügunspark	the theme park

das Restaurant	the restaurant
die Eisdiele	the ice cream parlor
der Imbiss	the food stand
der Rucksack	the backpack
das Zelt	the tent
der Schlafsack	the sleeping bag
der Strand	the beach
das Lagerfeuer	the bonfire
das Picknick	the picnic
der Flughafen	the airport
das Flugzeug	the plane
das Zimmer	the room
der Sitzplatz	the seat
das Hotel	the hotel
der Schlüssel	the key
der Koffer	the suitcase
die Passagiere	the passengers
der Reisepass	the passport
der Flug	the flight

die Ankunft	the arrival
die Kamera	the camera
der Abflug	the departure
das Gepack	the luggage
der Baseball	the baseball
der Basketball	the basketball
der Tennis	the Tennis
der Vollyball	the volleyball
der Fußball	the soccerball
das Tischtennis	the table tennis
der Baseballschläger	the baseball bat
die Mannschaft	the team
der Stadion	the stadium
der Helm	the helmet
der Handschuh	the glove
der Tennisschläger	the racket
Weihnachten	Christmas
Heiligabend	Christmas Eve
Ostern	Easter

Vatertag	Father's Day
Muttertag	Mother's Day
Sylvester	New Year's Eve
Chanukka	Hanukkah
Dreikönigstag	Three Kings' Day
Tag der Unabhängigkeit	Independence Day
Erntedankfest	Thanksgiving
Tag der Arbeit	Labor Day
die Hochzeit	the wedding
das Jubiläum	the anniversary
die Parade	the parade
das Kostüm	the costume
die Maske	the mask
das Feuerwerk	the fireworks
die Party	the party
das Geschenk	the gift
die Einladung	the invitation
der Tanz	the dance
das Konzert	the concert

Verbs:

German	English
Sport treiben	to play sports
schlafen	to sleep
Briefe schreiben	to write letters
lesen	to read
putzen	to clean
aufräumen	to pick up
Wäsche waschen	to wash laundry
Geschirr spülen	to wash dishes
fegen	to sweep
Staub saugen	to vacuum
besuchen	to visit
anschauen	to look at
einkaufen	to go shopping
Rad fahren	to ride a bicycle
Fotos machen	to take pictures
wandern	to hike
Gewichte heben	to lift weights

landen	to land
verpassen	to miss (a train or plane)
abfliegen	the take off
genießen	to enjoy
fliegen	to fly
kennenlernen	to get to know
reisen	to travel
jagen	to hunt
grillen	to grill
spazieren gehen	to go on a walk
wandern	to hike

Phrases:

German	English
Was machen wir?	What are we doing?
Was gibt es zu tun?	What is there to do?

Unit 9

Grammar: Modal Verbs

Modals verbs show up often in spoken German. For this reason, you will need to learn them well, and how to conjugate them. The problem with conjugating modals, is that they take an irregular conjugation pattern, even different from other irregular verbs.

Modal verbs are verbs that modify another verb. That means that you will almost always encounter them with another verb. For example: I sing, I can sing. You speak. You have to speak. He sleeps. He wants to sleep.

Most modal verbs undergo a vowel change in all of their singular forms. The modal verbs are as follows.

Infinite	1st and 3rd Person Singular	English
können	kann	to be able to, can
wollen	will	to want to
müssen	muss	to have to, must
sollen	soll	to ought to
dürfen	darf	to be allowed to

Be especially careful not to mix up **wollen** with **werden**. The singular form of wollen is "ich will", which sounds like the English words "I will". This instead means "I want". To say "I will", you need to say "Ich werde".

In German, the modal verb is usually in the regular verb position and is conjugated. The other verb that is being modified is placed in its infinitive form at the end of the sentence. Here are some examples that show how modal verbs work.

German	Literal English	Practical English
Ich kann Gitarre spielen.	I can guitar play.	I can play the guitar.
Du willst Kekse essen.	You want cookies eat.	You want to eat cookies.
Er muss jetzt lernen.	He must now learn.	He has to study now.
Sollen wir bald fahren?	Should we soon drive?	Should we drive soon?

Modal verbs do not add –e for1st person singular/ich or –t for 3rd person singular/er, sie, es. (Though don't forget the vowel change.) These are the only kind of verbs in which the 1st person and 3rd person singular forms are identical.

Modal verbs still add -st for the 2nd person singular form/du, though they undergo the same vowel change as the other singular forms. Compare the following examples.

Singular Forms

ich kann, muss, will

du kannst, musst, willst

Plural Forms

wir können, müssen, wollen

ihr könnt, müsst, wollt

er kann, muss, will   sie können, müssen, wollen

sie kann, muss, will   Sie können, müssen, wollen

es kann, muss, will

Now let's consider another similar verb. Mögen/to like is conjugated like modals. It is most correct to use mögen when talking about liking nouns and gern when talking about liking verbs. Take a look at the different forms in the following examples.

ich mag   wir mögen

du magst   ihr mögt

er mag   sie mögen

sie mag   Sie mögen

es mag

German	English
Ich mag Kuchen.	I like cake.
Wir mögen schnelle Autos.	We like fast cars.
Er mag die Katze.	He likes the cat.

The common verb **möchten** is a form of the verb mögen. Instead of meaning simply *to like*, it means *would like*. Using *wollen* to ask for something is not as polite as using möchten. It is especially important to use möchten in situations like ordering food at a restaurant. Compare the tone and meaning the following sentences.

German	English
Ich will ein Getränk.	I want a drink.
Ich möchte ein Getränk.	I would like a drink.
Er will ein Buch.	He wants a book.
Er möchte ein Buch.	He would like a book.
Sie will essen.	She wants to eat.
Sie möchte essen.	She would like to eat.

Pronunciation: IE vs. EI

The vowel combinations ie and ei are very common in German. They do not, however, act like they do in English, and often you will hear English speakers mispronounce German names because of these and similar vowel combination.

Luckily, there is a simple rule to remember how to pronounce each one: "When two vowels go walking, the second one does the talking." This means, that ie says "e", because the second letter is e, and ei says "i", because the second letter is i. There are many examples, including many common names, and here a few to practice.

German	English
lieben	to love
zwei	two
vier	four
sieben	seven
frei	free
langweilig	boring
Einstein	last name
Frankenstein	last name

Klein	short/last name
die Zwiebel	the onion
der Bleistift	the pencil
das Teil	the part
der Dieb	the thief
das Ziel	the goal

Culture: Politics

Germany has undergone many political changes over the years. The modern state of Germany is actually younger than the United States.

For hundreds of years, the area that now contains Germany, Austria and Switzerland, as well as areas that are now part of neighboring countries, were occupied by dozens of small kingdoms that had a similar culture and language.

This area was part of what was called the Holy Roman Empire from 962 AD to 1806 AD, and from 1919 – 1933 AD experimented with being a republic, called the Weimar Republic, which was the first time Germany existed in a form relative to the modern state. The Weimar Repulic ultimately failed, largely because of World War I and its aftermath.

In the government's poor state, Hitler and his Nazi Party rose to power, creating a government known as the Third Reich. This fell as a result of World War II, and Germany split into two countries: East Germany and West Germany.

The two conuntries remained apart for decades, until the fall of the Berlin Wall and reunification of Germany in 1989. Today, Germany remains united, and has a democratic government with many similarities to the United States with three branches of government.

The executive branch consists of a Chancellor and a President. The President is the figurehead of the country, much like the Queen in England. He or she reperents the country in politic situations or gatherings, but holds little actual power. The Chancellor, however, is the political leader of the country, much like the President of the United States.

The Legistative branch consists of two houses of Congress, the Bundestag and the Bundesrat. One represents the people and the other the German states. Instead of having a single Supreme Court in the Judicial Branch, they have a series of high courts, each of which deals with a certain topic.

Switzerland's government differs in that it is a direct democracy, where citizens introduce laws and then each law is voted on directly by the people. Such laws must gain at least 100,000 supporters before being put to a vote. Becoming a Swiss citizen is a long and difficult process and citizenship is highly prized among them.

They do not have a signal head of state, but an eight person Swiss Fedral Council, which serves as the executive branch of government. There is a President of this Council, but it is largely a ceremonial title.

Switzerland also had two houses of parliament: the Council of States, which represents the Cantons (states) of Switzerland and the National Council, with representatives elected by popular vote. They also have a Federal Supreme Court which hears appeals from the lower state courts.

The Government of Austria is similar to that of Germany, with a Chancellor and President, two chambers of parliament (The National Council and the Federal Council). Like Switzerland, citizens can start popular intitivaties that must be considered by parliament if they can gain support from 100,000 voters.

Unlike Germany and Switzerland, their judicial branch is completely at the federal level and there are no state courts.

Both Germany and Austria are participants in the European Union and the so-called "Euro Zone" of those who have adopted the Euro as currency. Switzerland remains outside the European Union and the Euro Zone and maintains strict international neutrality. They do not participate in any armed conflicts or provide special aid to any side of a conflict. For this reason, Switzerland has become a haven for money and refugees during times of conflict.

Vocabulary: Writing Letters/Technology

Nouns:

German	English
der Brief	the letter
die Post	the mail/the post office
der Briefträger	the mail carrier
der Gruß	the greeting
die Verabschiedung	the farewell
der Satz	the sentence
der Absatz	the paragraph
der Punkt	the period
das Komma	the comma
das Fragezeichen	the question mark
das Ausrufezeichen	the exclaimation point
die Frage	the question
die Briefmarke	the postage stamp
der Umschlag	the envelope
die Adresse	the address
das Postfach	the P.O. Box

die Postleitzahl	the zip code
die Strasse	the street
die Stadt	the city
der Anspitzer	the sharpener
der Kleber	the glue
der Hefter	the stapler
der Monitor	the monitor
die Maus	the mouse
das Netzwerk	the network
der Drucker	the printer
der Bildschirm	the screen
die Software	the software
die Webseite	the web page
die Webseiteadresse	the web address
das Fenster	the window
das Kennwort	the password
der Kopfhörer	the earphones
das Mikrophon	the microphone
der Benutzername	the username

der Klammeraffe	the at sign
die Kontakte	the contact
der Scanner	the scanner
der DVD Brenner	the DVD burner
der Computer	the computer
die Daten	the Data
die Festplatte	the hard drive
die E-Mail	the e-mail
der Ordner	the folder
die Startseite	the home page
das Internet	the Internet
der Laptop	the laptop
der Link	the link
der Briefkasten	the mailbox
der Akku	the recharable battery
die Eingabetaste	the enter key
die Leertaste	the space bar
die Suchmaschine	the search engine
der Anhang	the attachment

German	English
das Betriebssystem	the operating system
.de	German website extension
der Fehler	the error

Verbs:

German	**English**
schreiben	to write
erzählen	to tell a story
schicken	to send
grüßen	to greet
sich verabschieden	to bid farewell
danken	to thank
helfen	to help
vermissen	to miss
löschen	to erase
formatieren	to format
gehen zu	go to
installieren	to install
sich anmelden	to log in
sich abmelden	to log out

suchen	to look for
sich einloggen	to log in
sich auslogen	to log out
öffnen	to open
kopieren	to copy
einfügen	to paste
drucken	to print
neu starten	to reboot
speichern	to save
auswählen	to select
klicken	to click
im Internet surfen	to surf the Internet
eine Seite besuchen	to visit a site
einschalten	to turn on
abschalten	to turn off
schicken	to send
schließen	to close
ausschneiden	to cut
entfernen	to delete

| herunterladen | to download |
| bearbeiten | to edit |

Phrases:

German	**English**
Lieber Hans...	Dear Hans...
Liebe Gretel...	Dear Gretel...
Sehr geehrte(r) Herr/Frau	Most honored Mr./Mrs.
Mit freundlichen Grüßen	With friendly greetings
Alles Gute!	All the best!
Ich würde gerne wissen...	I would like to know...
Es freut mich zu hören, dass	I'm glad to hear that...
Vielen Dank!	Many thanks!

Unit 10

Grammar: Expressions of time

In German, word order makes more of a difference than it does in English. To speak in the best way, there is one rule to keep in mind:

First comes **time**, then comes **manner**, then comes **place**.

Not all sentences will include all of these elements, sometimes only one of them or two. Remember that even if you only have time and place that time still comes before place.

Time means something that tells you when the sentence takes place.

German	English
gestern	yesterday
heute	today
morgen	tomorrow
jetzt	now
später	later
in einer Stunde	in an hour
bald	soon

Manner tells you the way you do something.

German	English
mit dem Bus	with the bus
mit dem Kuli	with a pen
mit meinem Vater	with my father
zu Fuss	on foot

Place tells you where something is happening.

German	English
hier	here
dort	there
in der Stadt	in the city
zu Hause	at home
in der Schule	at school

Here are some example sentences. Though people will still understand you if you get these elements out of order, you will sound better if you put them in the correct order.

German

Wir fahren heute mit dem Bus in der/die Stadt.

Er schreibt jetzt mit dem Kuli.

Ich gehe morgen zu Fuss in die Schule.

English

We are driving today with the bus in the city.

He is writing now with the pen.

I am walking tomorrow to school on foot.

Prepositions with Expressions of Time

You use different prepositions before different kinds of expressions of time.

Before saying the time of day, use the preposition **um**.

German	English
um 12 Uhr	at twelve o'clock
um halb sechs	at five thirty
um Mitternacht	at midnight
um Viertel nach acht	at a quarter past eight
um Viertel vor sieben	at a quarter to seven

German	English
Wir spielen um 12 Uhr das Spiel.	We are playing the game at 12 o'clock.
Ich gehe um acht zur Schule.	I am going to school at eight.

Sie isst um Mittag Mittagessen.   She eats lunch at noon.

When you are talking about a day of the week, use the preposition *am* (an + dem).

German	English
am Sonntag	on Sunday
am Montag	on Monday
am Dienstag	on Tuesday
am Mittwoch	on Wednesday
am Donnerstag	on Thursday
am Freitag	on Friday
am Samstag	on Saturday

German	English
Kommen Sie am Freitag vorbei.	Come by on Friday.
Machen wir am Montag einen Termin.	Let's make an appointment on Monday
Er dient am Donnerstag.	He serves on Thursday.

When you are talking about a month of the year, use the preposition *im* (in + dem).

German	English
im Januar	in January

im Februar	in February
im März	in March
im April	in April
im Mai	in May
im Juni	in June
im Juli	in July
im August	in August
im September	in September
im Oktober	in October
im November	in November
im Dezember	in December

German	English
Ich habe im März Geburtstag.	My birthday is in March.
Er geht im Juli auf Mission.	He is going on a mission in July.
Wir feiern im April Ostern.	We celebrate Easter in April.

When you are talking about years, there are two different ways you can use. The first way is to say **im Jahre** and then the year, although this is sort of an old-fashioned and formal way of saying it. The second way to put the year without using any preposition.

German	English
im Jahre 1800	in the year 1800
im Jahre 1984	in the year 1984
im Jahre 2012	in the year 2012

German	English
Ich wurde 1983 geboren.	I was born in 1983.
Ich wurde im Jahre 1999 geboren.	I was born in the year 1999.
Die Kirche wurde 1830 gegründet.	The church was founded in 1830.

It is important to learn the ordinal forms of the numbers when talking about dates as well. Just like in English, you don't say the "two of August" but the "2nd of August". The following is a list of all the ordinal numbers you will need for dates. Notice that the most irregular ones are "first", "second" and "third", and the rest are much closer to their other form.

Also notice that the numbers after 19 take a slightly different form, with an additional "s" in them.

German	English
der erste	the first
der zweite	the second

der dritte	the third
der vierte	the forth
der fünfte	the fifth
der sechste	the sixth
der siebte	the seventh
der achte	the eighth
der neunte	the ninth
der zehnte	the tenth
der elfte	the eleventh
der zwölfte	the twelveth
der dreizehnte	the thirteenth
der vierzehnte	the fourteenth
der fünfzehnte	the fifteenth
der sechzehnte	the sixteenth
der siebzehnte	the seventeenth
der achtzehnte	the eighteenth
der neunzehnte	the nineteenth
der zwanzigste	the twentieth
der einundzwanzigste	the twenty-first

German	English
der zweiundzwanzigste	the twenty-second
der dreiundzwanzigste	the twenty-third
der vierundzwanzigste	the twenty-fourth
der fünfundzwanzigste	the twenty-fifth
der sechsundzwanzigste	the twenty-sixth
der siebenundzwanzigste	the twenty-seventh
der achtundzwanzigste	the twenty-eighth
der neunundzwanzigste	the twenty-ninth
der dreißigste	the thirteth
der einunddreißigste	the thirty-first

When talking about a date, including a baptismal one, you should use the preposition "am" and add an "n" at the end of the date, because "am" is dative and dates need to take normal adjective endings.

German
English

Er wird am ersten Mai kommen.	He will come on May 1st.
Die Taufe findet am vierten statt.	The baptism is taking place on the 4th.
Ich habe am achtzehnten Geburtstag.	My birthday is on the eighteenth.

Pronunciation: AU, ÄU and EU

German is more consistent on how vowel combinations sound, and learning them will help you greatly. Vowels with umlauts are not often combined with other vowels, but A umlaut does have one expection to this.

Both ÄU and EU make the same sound--a sound like the final sound in the English word toy.

German	English
die Freude	the joy
treu	loyal
scheu	shy
das Fräulein	the little girl
die Häuser	the houses
die Mäuser	the mice

Without an umlaut, AU sounds like the vowel sound in the English word *bow*, such as in 'The singer took a bow after his performance' and not like the weapon used in archery. Be sure not to mix the two combinations up, because they will change the meaning. Often, it is the difference between singular and plural.

German	English
die Frau	the woman
blau	blue
der Stau	the traffic

Culture: German Pastimes

German speakers enjoy a variety of pastimes, similar to those in the United States. Sports are an integral part of their lifestyle, though they focus on differents sports than in the United States. Baseball and Basketball are much rarer, and soccer much more popular. German speakers often organize soccer clubs, called Fußball Klubs, in their towns that compete against each other.

Almost every large German city has a local professional soccer team with a matching stadium. Germany also has an official soccer team called the Bundesliga, which competes with other national teams in competitions like the World Cup.

The team from Munich is called FC. Bayern München, and is the most wealthy team in Germany, and so draws many star players. This brings a division among Germans, some of who love the team and others who cannot stand it.

Many German-speakers also enjoy traveling. An excellent transportation network of trains, planes and busses makes it easy and inexpensive to travel Europe. Because much of Europe belongs to the European union, travelers do not have to show their passports when going from one European Union country to another. Many German-speakers also like vacationing in the United States. Chances are that when you visit a popular tourist attraction in the U.S., you will probably run into a few German speakers.

Many German speakers simply vacation in their own country. Though many of them love the outdoors, hunting, fishing and camping are strictly regulated. One beloved activity is hiking or wandern, and with all of the scenic trails, it is easy to see why. In some areas, people organize hiking clubs that undertake regular hikes along a variety of trails. Some of these clubs wear traditional clothing while they hike and carry large, carved walking sticks.

Though there are many old buildings, castles, cathedreals and fortress, some of which date back to Medieval and even Roman times, most German speakers are not as interested in these sights, because they are more commonplace than in places like the United States. These sites, however, draw many tourists, including missionaries on their preparation day.

Many German speakers are fond of open air markets. You will likely see weekly or monthly farmers markets as well as markets set up for special occasions such as Christmas or Karneval.

German-speaking countries are also home to many fine musical groups, from cathedral choirs to famous orchestras. Many of the great composers of Western music throughout history have come from German-speaking countries, such as Bach, Mozart, Beethoven, Brahms, Haydn, Wager, Strauss and Schubert. Their legacy is alive and well today in the concert halls and opera houses through Germany, Austria, and Switzerland.

Vocabulary: Breakfast

Nouns:

German	English
das Brot	the bread
das Brötchen	the roll
der Schinken	the ham
der Käse	the cheese
die Milch	the milk
die Marmelade	the jam
die Butter	the butter
das Müsli	the granola
der Joghurt	the yogurt
das Ei	the egg
der Saft	the juice
der Orangensaft	the orange juice
die Wurst	the sausage
der Speck	the bacon

Verbs:

German	English
essen	to eat
trinken	to drink
frühstücken	to eat breakfast
kochen	to cook
grillen	to grill
braten	to roast
fritieren	to fry
frieren	to freeze
hitzen	to heat
gießen	to pour

Phrases:

German	English
Was essen Sie zum Frühstück?	What do you want to eat for breakfast?

Unit 11

Grammar: Comparatives and Superlatives

Comparatives are forms of adjectives that you use to compare to nouns, like bigger, faster, and taller. Good news for English speakers—making comparatives in German shouldn't be any trouble. Just like in English, all you have to do is add –er. In fact, it is even simplifier than English. In English, there are other rules for longer adjectives. In German, you add –er to the end no matter how long the adjective is.

The only thing that might give you a problem is that sometimes the adjectives add an umlaut in the comparative form. In this case, look for adjective that have a, o, u or au, and most of the time, you should add the umlaut.

Here are some examples of adjectives and their comparative forms:

German	English
heiß – heißer	hot – hotter
kalt – kälter	cold – colder
groß – größer	tall – taller
klein – kleiner	small – smaller
interessant – interessanter	interesting – more interesting

klug – klüger	smart – smarter
langsam – langsamer	slow – slower
schnell – schneller	fast – faster

Superlatives are forms of adjectives that talk about something that is the best or the most like biggest, fastest and tallest. These forms are a little trickier, though still usually follow set patterns. There are two ways you can use this form. You can either add the word am (which is a contraction of an and dem) before the word and then add –sten to the end of the adjective, or you can use the article of the noun in front of the adjective, add –st and then add the usual adjective endings.

The simpiliest way is the first way, so when in doubt, use that one. Here are some examples of both ways.

With the Article and Adjective Endings

German

Er ist der beste Missionar.

Bruder Krause ist der größte Mann der Gemeinde.

Mein Fahrrad ist das schnellste.

English

He is the best missionary.

Brother Krause is the tallest man in the ward.

My bike is the fastest.

With am and -sten

German

Schwester Fuchs ist am besten.

Frau Fischer ist am kleinsten.

Mein Auto ist am schnellsten.

English

Sister Fuchs is the best.

Mrs. Fischer is the shortest.

My car is the fastest.

Pronunciation: SP, SCH, ST

The letter S usually sounds like the English letter Z when it is in the beginning or the middle of a word. When it is found at the end of word, it sounds like the English letter S.

When S is paired with other conssonants, however, it can make different sounds. The most common combinations with S are SP, SCH, and ST.

The letter combination SP is usually only found at the beginnings of words, though you will occasionally see it in the middle. It makes a sounds like the English combination SHP, without any hint of Z. Here are a few examples:

German	English
spielen	to play
sprechen	to speak
spenden	to donate
der Spass	the fun
der Spiegel	the mirror
der Sprengstoff	the explosives

The letter combination SCH can appear in many different places in a word and sounds like the English combination SH. Here are some examples:

German	English
der Busch	the bush
der Tisch	the table
der Wunsch	the wish
das Schach	chess
der Schädel	the skull
der Schinken	the ham

The letter combination ST is often found at the beginning of words and sounds like the English letter combination SHT. Here are a few examples:

German	English
stechen	to sting
streiten	to fight
stehlen	to steal
der Stab	the stick
die Stadt	the city
das Stadion	the stadium
der Stadtteil	the city district
der Strand	the beach

Culture: The Metric System

The metric system is a system of measurement that has been adopted almost everywhere in the world except for the United States and a few other countries. Germany, Austria and Switzerland all use the metric system, and so if you are from the United States, you will have to rethink measurement completely.

Much of the metric system's popularity likely stems from the fact that it is simple to use. All units of measurement are based on powers of 10, which makes it simple to convert from unit of measurement to another. Some metric units, such as liters and centimeters, are already used often in the United States and so you might not have such a hard time with them.

Learning the prefixes of the metric system will help you figure out units of measurement quickly. Pay attention to the symbols as well, as most often the measurements are written with symbols instead of full words.

Text	Symbol	Factor
tera	T	1000000000000
giga	G	1000000000
mega	M	1000000
kilo	k	1000
hecto	h	100
(none)	(none)	1
deci	d	0.1
centi	c	0.01
milli	m	0.001
micro	μ	0.000001
nano	n	0.000000001

The following section breaks down different units of measurement within the metric system and where you will likely encounter them in German-speaking countries. Many of the units you will not encounter in everyday life, but it is good to know them for practice.

Units of Distance

The unit for distance in the metric system is meters. When looking on a map, remember that distances are given in kilometers, which are much smaller than miles.

Text	Symbol	Factor
terameter	Tm	1000000000000
gigameter	Gm	1000000000
megameter	Mm	1000000
kilometer	km	1000
hectometer	hm	100
meter	m	1
decimeter	dm	0.1
centimeter	cm	0.01
millimeter	mm	0.001
micrometer	μm	0.000001
nanometer	nm	0.000000001

Units of Speed

The metric system uses kilometers per hour instead of miles per hour. When you are driving, your speedometer will show your speed in kilometers per hour, and the speed limit signs will be shown with these same units.

Text	Symbol	Factor
terameters/Stunde	Tm/S	1000000000000
gigameters/Stunde	Gm/S	1000000000
megameters/Stunde	Mm/S	1000000
kilometers/Stunde	km/S	1000
hectometers/Stunde	hm/S	100
meters/Stunde	m/S	1
decimeters/Stunde	dm/S	0.1
centimeters/Stunde	cm/S	0.01
millimeters/Stunde	mm/S	0.001
micrometers/Stunde	μm/S	0.000001
nanometers/Stunde	nm/S	0.000000001

Units of Volume

Volume is measured in liters in the metric system, which is one metric measure that is seen often in the United States, especially when measuring liquids like soda. Keep in mind that all liquids in German-speaking countries are measured in liters, including gasoline. When the prices as teh pump look low, remember that it takes more than three liters to equal a single gallon.

Text	Symbol	Factor
teraliter	Tl	1000000000000
gigaliter	Gl	1000000000
megaliter	Ml	1000000
kiloliter	kl	1000
hectoliter	hl	100
liter	l	1
deciliter	dl	0.1
centiliter	cl	0.01
milliliter	ml	0.001
microliter	μl	0.000001
nanoliter	nl	0.000000001

Units of Mass

Mass is measured in grams in the metric system. When you are making a recipe, it will often call for grams or kilograms of certain ingredients. People also talk about their weight in kilograms, which are much heavier than pounds.

Text	Symbol	Factor
teragram	Tg	1000000000000

gigagram	Gg	1000000000
megagram	Mg	1000000
kilogram	kg	1000
hectogram	hg	100
gram	g	1
decigram	dg	0.1
centigram	cg	0.01
milligram	mg	0.001
microgram	µg	0.000001
nanogram	ng	0.000000001

Units of Area

All unit of area are two-dimensional, and so much be measured in "square" measurements. This is indicated by putting a small number two next to the symbol.

Text	Symbol	Factor
square tetrameter	Tm^2	1000000000000
square gigameter	Gm^2	1000000000
square megameter	Mm^2	1000000
square kilometer	km^2	1000

square hectometer	hm^2	100
square meter	m^2	1
square decimeter	dm^2	0.1
square centimeter	cm^2	0.01
square millimeter	mm^2	0.001
square micrometer	μm^2	0.000001
square nanometer	nm^2	0.000000001

Vocabulary: Lunch and Dinner

Nouns:

German	English
das Mittagessen	the lunch
das Abendessen	the dinner
der Teller	the plate
das Glas	the glass
der Löffel	the spoon
das Messer	the knife
die Gabel	the fork
das Fleisch	the meat
das Brot	the bread
die Butter	the butter
der Käse	the cheese
der Reis	the rice
das Ei	the egg
das Gemüse	the vegatable
der Nachtisch	the dessert
das Getränk	the drink

die Soße	the sauce
die Nudeln	the noodles
die Torte	the pie
der Kuchen	the cake
die Kekse	the cookies
der Pudding	the pudding
der Zucker	the sugar
das Salz	the salt
der Pfeffer	the pepper
der Knoblauch	the garlic
der Apfel	the apple
die Banane	the banana
die Traube	the grape
die Zitrone	the lemon
die Orange	the orange
die Mango	the mango
der Pfirsich	the peach
die Ananas	the pineapple
die Birne	the pear

die Erdbeere	the strawberry
die Wassermelone	the watermelon
die Avokado	the avocado
die Bohne	the bean
die Kirsche	the cherry
der Brokkoli	the broccoli
die Karotte	the carrot
die Tomate	the tomato
der Mais	the corn
die Zwiebel	the onion
der Saft	the juice
das Rindfleisch	the beef
das Hähnchen	the chicken (food)
der Fisch	the fish
die Meeresfrüchte	the seafood (except for fish)
das Schweinefleisch	the pork
der Schinken	the ham
der Speck	the bacon
das Steak	the steak

Verbs:

German	English
essen	to eat
Hunger haben	to be hungry
Durst haben	to be thirsty
trinken	to drink
einladen	to invite
abräumen	to clean up
den Tisch decken	to set the table
sich hinsetzen	to sit down
kochen	to cook
backen	to bake
würzen	to season
gießen	to pour
danken	to thank
schneiden	to cut
kauen	to chew

Adjectives

German	English
bitter	bitter
warm	warm
gefroren	frozen
roh	raw
süß	sweet
frisch	fresh
scharf	spicy
lecker/köstlich	delicious
salzig	salty

Phrases:

German	English
Guten Apetit!	Good apetite!
Lasst's euch schmecken!	Enjoy your meal!
Schmeckt es?	Does it taste good?
Prost!	Cheers!
Zum Wohl!	To your health!

Unit 12

Grammar: Conversational Past Tense

There are two forms of past tense in German: conversational past and narrative past, sometimes called the simple past. The conversational past tense is used in everyday speech and writing, while the narrative past is used mostly for telling stories. Some regions of German-speaking countries, especially in Austria, do not use the narrative past at all.

The pattern for the conversational past tense involves two parts. The first part is the conjugated form of one of two helping verbs: **haben** or **sein**. The second part is a past participle, which is a form of the verb you want to be in past tense.

First, let's consider the two helping verbs and how to decide which one to use. The helping verb haben is used a majority of the time, so, when in doubt, use it. Be sure to remember that haben conjugates irregularly. Here's a chart to refresh your memory:

Singular	English	Plural	English
ich habe	I have	wir haben	we have
du hast	you have (I)	ihr habt	you all have
er hat	he has	sie haben	they have

sie hat she has   Sie haben   you have (F)

es hat   it has

Sein is used only for certain verbs of motion such as to go, to walk, to run, to fly, to jump, to drive, etc. It also used by a handful of verbs that talk about a person's state such as **bleiben**/to stay, **sterben**/to die, and **sein**/to be. All **sein** verbs must be intransitive, which means that they do not take a direct object. Some verbs can take either **haben** or **sein** depending on whether they take a direct object or not.

A good example of a verb like this is fahren/to drive. When you use fahren to say that you drove from one place to another, it does not take a direct object and so uses sein. When you use fahren to say that you drove a vehicle such as a car, it does have a direct object and so uses haben as a helping verb. Compare the following two sentences.

German

Ich bin nach Ulm gefahren.

I drove to Ulm.   (No direct object)

English

Ich habe mein Auto nach Ulm gefahren.

I drove my car to Ulm.   (Auto is the direct object)

One good way to check is to see whether an action could take you from one place to another. If it can, it is probably takes a sein helping verb. Sein also has an irregular conjugation, even more than haben. Here is a chart to review it:

Singular	English	Plural	English
ich bin	I am	wir sind	we are
du bist	you are (I)	ihr seid	you all are (I)
er ist	he is	sie sind	they are
sie ist	she is	Sie sind	you are (F)
es ist	it is		

Now, let's think about the past participle. The second verb is in its past participle form and is at the end of the sentence or clause.

To form a past participle, insert ge- in front of the verb stem (made by dropping the –en off of the infinitive form of the verb such as mach for the verb machen) and then either –t or –en at the end of the stem.

There is only one past participle for each verb. Past participles of irregular verbs usually end in –en and even some regular present tense verbs have irregular past participles. Some irregular verbs change the vowel sound in the past participle as well. It is something about a verb you should memorize. See what patterns you can notice in the following examples.

Infinitive	Helping Verb	Past Participle	English
spielen	haben	gespielt	played
fahren	sein	gefahren	drove
lachen	haben	gelacht	laughed
essen	haben	gegessen	ate
machen	haben	gemacht	made
lesen	haben	gelesen	read
sagen	haben	gesagt	said
sprechen	haben	gesprochen	spoke
fragen	haben	gefragt	asked
gehen	sein	gegangen	went
trinken	haben	getrunken	drank

Here are some example sentences that include regular past tense conjugation. Notice that even though you use the verbs haben and sein in German, you do not include them in your English translation.

German	English
Der Untersucher hat uns gefragt.	The investigator asked us.
Der Junge hat das Gebet gesagt.	The boy said the prayer.

Er hat einen Termin gemacht.	He made an appointment.
Der Bischof hat gelacht.	The bishop laughed.
Heute, haben sie ein Brettspiel gespielt.	Today, they played a board game.

Here are some examples of sentences that include irregular past tense conjugation.

German	**English**
Ich habe den Saft getrunken.	I drank the juice.
Der Vater is in die Kirche gegangen.	The father went to church.
Wir haben nur Deutsch gesprochen.	We only spoke German.
Er hat im Buch Mormon gelesen.	He read in the Book of Mormon.
Zum Mittagessen, haben wir Wurst gegessen.	For lunch, we ate sausage.
Du bist nach Ulm versetzt worden	You were transferred to Ulm.

Pronunciation: A Umlaut

A is one of three letters that can take an umlaut in addition to O and U. An alternate way to make the same sound is by writing ae. Adding an umlaut completely changes the sound of the vowel, and can be a little harder for English speakers to master, although A umlaut is the easiest of the trio, because we do use similar sounds in English. All umlauts create vowels that are pronounced in the front of the mouth.

The A umlaut makes a sound similar to the vowel in the English word get, which makes it easier than O or U umlaut. There are two kinds of A umlaut sounds: short and long. Take a look at a few examples of words with the short A umlaut sound.

German	English
die Männer	the men
die Hände	the hands
die Bänke	the benches
die Schränke	the wardrobes
die Äpfel	the apples

The long A umlaut is the same sound held longer. It is often used when A umlaut is followed by the letter H. Compare some examples of words with the long

A umlaut sound.

German	English
das Mädchen	the girl
wählen	to vote
die Währung	the currency

If an A umlaut is followed by a U, a complete different sound is produced this is similar to the vowel sound in the English word toy, or the German vowel combination eu. Here are a few examples of this happening.

German	English
die Häuser	the houses
das Fräulein	the young woman
die Kräuter	the herbs

Culture: **Money in German-Speaking Countries**

For many years, Germany used the Deutschmark/Pfennig as its currency. These coins and bills all featured famous German figures and buildings. With the advent of the European Union, however, Germany and Austria both adopted the Euro as their currency. The Euro bills feature buildings from different European countries. There are no one Euro bills, but instead one and two Euro coins. Each of these coins features an image from the country in which they were minted.

Euro bills differ from dollars, in that each denomination is a different color and size, growing larger as the denomination grows larger. Euros are broken down into cents, where 100 cents is equal to one Euro. Some Euro coins, such as the 50-cent piece, have ridges along the edge to help identify them among other coins.

The rate of exchange between Euros and dollars fluctuates every day, but usually, the Euro is worth more than the dollar. Keep that in mind when spending Euros.

Switzerland refused to join the European Union, and also did not adopt the Euro. Instead, they keep their currency, known as the Swiss Franc.

Austria's traditional currency was called the Krone,

and then the Schilling. It now uses the Euro like Germany.

Value	Form	Color	Picture
1 cent	coin	copper	Europe
2 cents	coin	copper	Europe
5 cents	coin	copper	Europe
10 cents	coin	gold	Europe
20 cents	coin	gold	Europe
50 cents	coin	gold	Europe
1 Euro	coin	gold/silver	Europe
2 Euro	coin	gold/silver	Europe
5 Euro	bill	blue	Classical architecture
10 Euro	bill	red	Romanesque architecture
20 Euro	bill	blue	Gothic architecture
50 Euro	bill	orange	Renaissance architecture
100 Euro	bill	green	Baroque architecture
200 Euro	bill	yellow	Art Nouveau architecture
500 Euro	bill	purple	Modern architecture

One of the interesting features of the Euro is that each country mints their own coins and gets to choose what to feature on the back of the coin. All of the coins have a picture of Europe on one side.

Each country chooses images of people, events,

symbols, or buildings that are important to them and uses these on their coins. Some countries even mint limited edition coins from their country in honor of special events or milestones. Even Vatican City has its own kind of Euro coins featuring a picture of the Pope.

See how many different countries you can collect while you are in Europe. There are seventeen members of the "Eurozone", or nations that have adopted the Euro, so there are many different designs to collect.

Vocabulary: Clothing

Nouns:

German	English
der Gürtel	the belt
die Bluse	the blouse
die Krawatte	the tie
die Stiefel	the boots
die Mütze	the cap
der Mantel	the coat
das Kleid	the dress
der Hut	the hat
die Jacke	the jacket
der Pulli	the sweater
das Tshirt	the Tshirt
das Sweatshirt	the sweatshirt
der Badeanzug	the swimsuit
die Unterwäsche	the underwear
die Jeans	the jeans
die Hose	the pants

das Hemd	the shirt
die Schuhe	the shoes
die kurze Hose	the shorts
der Rock	the skirt
die Socken	the socks
der Anzug	the suit
der Ring	the ring
die Ohrringe	the earrings
die Stiefel	the boots
die Halskette	the necklace
die Brille	the glasses
die Sonnenbrille	the sunglasses
die Weste	the vest
der Knopf	the button
der Reißverschluss	the zipper
die Hosentasche	the pants pocket
die Strumpfhose	the pantyhose
die Wäsche	the laundry
der Schal	the scarf

die Kette	the necklace
der Ärmel	the sleeve
der Stoff	the fabric
die Baumwolle	the cotton
die Wolle	the wool
die Seide	the silk
das Leder	the leather
die Größe	the size

Verbs:

German	English
anprobieren	to try on
einkaufen gehen	to go shopping
sich anziehen	to get dressed
sich umziehen	to change clothes
sich ausziehen	to get undressed
tragen	to wear
waschen	to wash
wählen	to choose

suchen	to look for
verkaufen	to sell
ändern	to alter
nähen	to sew
flicken	to mend

Adjectives:

German	**English**
weich	soft
hart	hard
eng	tight
locker	loose
kurz	short
lang	long
elegant	elegant
modisch	fashionable
klein	small
mittelgroß	medium
groß	large

Phrases:

German	English
Steht es mir gut?	Does that look good on me?
Das steht dir gut.	That looks good on you.
Wie viel kostet es?	How much does it cost?
Welche Größe?	What size?
Welche Farbe?	What color?
Was tragen Sie?	What are you wearing?

Unit 13

Grammar: Simple Past Tense

There are two common ways to put verbs in the past tense. The conversational past uses a helping verb and the form used most often and in most German-speaking areas. Simple past or narrative past is a past tense form with no helping verb. This past tense form is used when writing or telling stories. It sometimes called simple past, because it is easier to form. It does not include any additional words and the word order is exactly the same as present tense. Remember that some German-speaking areas use the simple past tense only rarely or not at all.

Compare the three following forms of the same sentence.

Ich lerne und spreche Deutsch.	Present tense
Ich habe Deutsch gelernt und gesprochen.	Present perfect (past)
Ich lernte und sprach Deutsch.	Simple past

The simple past of regular verbs always follows the pattern of taking the verb stem and adding -te. Add an additional -st when conjugating with du, a –t for ihr, and an –n for wir and Sie. Here are a few examples of regular past tense verbs.

German

Ich arbeitete, lernte und lachte.

Du arbeitetest, lerntest und lachtest.

Er/sie arbeitete, lernte und lachte.

Wir arbeiteten, lernten und lachten.

Ihr arbeitetet, lerntet und lachtet.

English

I worked, learned and laughed.

You worked, learned and laughed.

He/She worked, learned and laughed.

We worked, learned and laughed.

You all worked, learned and laughed.

English	Simple Past	Conversational Past
played	spielte	gespielt
laughed	lachte	gelacht
made	machte	gemacht
learned	lernte	gelernt
cooked	kochte	gekocht
bought	kaufte	gekauft
worked	arbeitete	gearbeitet
served	diente	gedient
had	hatte	gehabt

The simple past of irregular verbs have different forms that must be memorized. These changes occur in the vowel sounds. Notice that there are no endings for the ich and er/sie/es forms, though the usual endings are given for the other forms: add an additional -st for du, a –t for ihr, and an –n for wir and Sie:

Ich trank, schrieb, fuhr las und war.

I drank, wrote, drove, read and was.

Du trankst, schriebst, fuhrst, last und warst.

You drank, wrote, drove, read and were.

Er/Sie/Es trank, schrieb, fuhr, las und war.

He/She/It drank, wrote, drove, read and was.

Wir tranken, schrieben, fuhren, lasen und waren.

We drank, wrote, drove, read and were.

Ihr trankt, schriebt, fuhrt und wart.

You all drank, wrote, drove, read and were.

English	Simple Past	Conversational Past
drank	trank	getrunken
ate	aß	gegessen
wrote	schrieb	geschrieben
drove	fuhr	gefahren
read	las	gelesen
slept	schlief	geschlafen
died	starb	gestorben
helped	half	geholfen
went	ging	gegangen
ran	lief	gelaufen
sang	sang	gesungen
was	war	gewesen

German	English
Ihr hattet nicht viel Geld.	You guys didn't have much money.
Waren Sie mal in Europa?	Were you (F) ever in Europe?
Sie erinnerte sich an mich.	She remembered me.
Du kauftest dir ein tolles Hemd.	You bought yourself a cool shirt.
Meine Mutter schnitt das Brot.	My mom cut the bread.

Wir putzten das Fenster.	We washed the window.
Ich sah den Film schon.	I saw the film already.
Du spieltest echt gut.	You played really well.
Wir zogen uns schnell um.	We changed clothes quickly.
Als ich klein war, hatte ich ein Dreirad.	When I was small, I had a tricycle.
Sie schrie, als sie den Hund sah.	She screamed as she saw the dog.
Er wusste, dass er mehr lernen sollte.	He knew that he should learn more.

Pronunciation: O Umlaut

O is one of three letters that can take an umlaut in addition to A and U. Another way to produce this sound is to write oe. Adding an umlaut completely changes the sound of the vowel and all umlauts create vowels that are pronounced in the far front of the mouth with rounded lips.

O umlaut does not have an equivalent sound in English, so you will probably need to practice this sound for a while before mastering it. Listen to native speakers and try to adopt not only the sound, but the way they shape their mouths for the best results.

There are two kinds of O umlaut sounds: short and long. Here are some examples of words with the short O umlaut sound.

German	English
der Löffel	the spoon
die Stöcke	the sticks
die Öffnung	the opening

The long O umlaut is the same sound held longer. It is often used when O umlaut is followed by the letter H. Here are some examples of words with the long O umlaut sound.

German	English
die Flöte	flute
böse	evil
die Söhne	sons

Culture: German Geography

The boundaries of what is now Germany have changed much over the years. The country of Germany is made up of what used to be dozens of small kingdoms that shared a common cultural heritage. Parts of what is now France, Austria, Czechoslovakia, Poland, and other countries have, at one time, been a part of Germany. These regions still exhibit a strong German influence.

Even more recently, Germany as split into two countries: communist East Germany and democratic West Germany. Even though the countries came back together into one on October 3rd, 1990, there are still noticeable cultural, linguistic and architectural differences between the two regions of Germany.

German is about 357,021 square kilometers large and about 82,000,000 people live there. It is the largest and strongest economy in Europe and a strong player in the European Union. It is split up into 16 smaller states or *Bundesländer* each with its own dialects and customs. Some states, like Bavaria, are very large and populous, while others consist of practically only a single large city, like Hamburg and Berlin.

State	Capital	Area (km²)	Population
Baden-Württemberg/Baden-Wurttemberg	Stuttgart	35,752	10,753,880
Bavaria/Bayern	Munich	70,549	12,538,696
Berlin/Berlin	Berlin	892	3,460,725
Brandenburg/Brandenburg	Potsdam	29,477	2,503,273
Bremen/Bremen	Bremen	404	660,999
Hamburg/Hamburg	Hamburg	755	1,786,448
Hesse/Hessen	Wiesbaden	21,115	6,067,021
State	Capital	Area (km²)	Population
Mecklenburg-Vorpommern/Mecklenburg-Vorpommern	Schwerin	23,174	1,642,327

State	Capital	Area (km²)	Population
Lower Saxony/NiederSaxon	Hanover	47,618	7,918,293
North Rhine-Westphalia/Nordrhein-Westpfalen	Düsseldorf	34,043	17,845,154
Rhineland-Palatinate/Rheinland-Pfalz	Mainz	19,847	4,003,745
Saarland/Saarland	Saarbrücken	2,569	1,017,567
Saxony/Saxon	Dresden	18,416	4,149,477
Saxony-Anhalt/Saxon-Anhalt	Magdeburg	20,445	2,335,006
Schleswig-Holstein/Schleswig-Holstein	Kiel	15,763	2,834,259
Thuringia/Thuringen	Erfurt	16,172	2,235,025

Source =
http://en.wikipedia.org/wiki/States_of_Germany

Vocabulary: In an Apartment

Nouns:

German	English
das Wohnzimmer	the living room
das Schlafzimmer	the bedroom
das Esszimmer	the dining room
das Badezimmer	the bathroom
das Treppenhaus	the stairwell
die Garage	the garage
die Küche	the kitchen
der Dachboden	the attic
der Keller	the cellar
der Garten	the garden
die Tür	the door
das Fenster	the window
der Klingel	the doorbell
der Teppich	the carpet
der Tisch	the table
der Schreibtisch	the desk

der Stuhl	the chair
das Sofa	the sofa
der Sessel	the recliner
der Schrank	the cupboard
die Schublade	the drawer
das Bett	the bed
das Kissen	the pillow
die Decke	the comforter
der Herd	the stove
der Ofen	the oven
der Mikrowellenherd	the microwave
die Waschmaschine	the washing machine
der Trockner	the dryer
das Bücherregal	the bookcase
der Fernseher	the television
die Kommode	the dresser
das Telefon	the telephone
das Bad	the bath
die Dusche	the shower

German	English
die Geschirrspülmachine	the dishwasher
der Spiegel	the mirror
die Seife	the soap
die Bürste	the brush
der Kamm	the comb
das Toilettenpapier	the toilet paper
die Zahnbürste	the toothbrush
die Zahnpasta	the toothpaste
der Rasierer	the razor
die Rasierkrem	the shaving cream
das Rasierwasser	the aftershave
das Duftwasser	the perfume
das Haarspray	the hairspray
das Deo(dorant)	the deodorant
das Waschbecken	the sink
der Wecker	the alarm clock
die Steroanlage	the stereo
der Fußboden	the floor
der Vorhang	the curtain

German	English
die Hausarbeit	the housework
der Lappen	the rag
der Besen	the broom
der Staubsauger	the vacuum
der Wischlappen	the mop
der Schwamm	the sponge
die Seife	the soap

Verbs:

German	English
putzen	to clean
wohnen	to live
aufräumen	to straighten up
einschlafen	to go to sleep
aufwachen	to wake up
beten	to pray
essen	to eat
mieten	to rent
das Bett machen	to make the bed
fegen	to sweep

staubsaugen	to vacuum
den Müll rausbringen	to take out the trash
die Wäsche waschen	to do the laundry
bügeln	to iron
abstauben	to dust
abwaschen	to do the dishes

Unit 14

Grammar: Future Tense

Fortunately, forming the future tense in German is much simpler than forming the past tense. There are a couple different ways to form the future tense in German, though each of them are simple, because you do not have to learn new forms of verbs as in the past tense.

The first way to speak of future tense, or things that are going to happen, is to use present tense and then add a specific time in the future. Let's take a look at some examples.

German

Wir fahren nächste Woche nach Frankfurt.

Du gehst morgen zur Zonenkonferenz.

Er spielt Volleyball diesen Sommer.

English

We are driving next week to Frankfurt.

You are going to zone conference tomorrow.

He plays volleyball this summer.

The other way to speak of future tense is to use two verbs. The first verb that is conjugated is werden/to become. It is an irregular verb and is conjugated as follows:

ich werde   wir werden

du wirst   ihr werdet

er wird   sie werden

sie wird   Sie werden

es wird

The other verb is then placed at the end of the sentence or clause in its infinitive form like using a modal verb. Take a look at some examples.

German

Wir werden nach Frankfurt fahren.

Du wirst zum Zonenkonferenz Kino gehen.

Er wird Fußball spielen.

English

We are going to drive to Frankfurt.

You are going to Zone Conference.

He is going to play soccer.

Pronunciation: U Umlaut

Along with O and A, U is one of three letters that can take an umlaut to change its sound. It is the same as writing the vowel combination ue. You might see this in people with the last name of Mueller. Chances are that their ancestors were actually called Müller, but that they changed it when entering another country. Adding an umlaut completely changes the sound of the vowel. All umlauts create vowels that are pronounced in the far front of the mouth, and that require rounded lips.

U umlaut can be tricky for English speakers, because it does not have an equivalent sound in English. There are two kinds of U umlaut sounds: short and long. Take a look at a few examples of words with the short U umlaut sound.

German	English
das Stück	the piece
die Brücke	the bridge
die Münze	the coin

The long U umlaut is the same sound held longer. It is often used when U umlaut is followed by the letter H. It is also sometimes written as the letter Y, especially in words borrowed from other languages. Here are some examples of words with the long U umlaut sound.

German	English
früh	early
grün	green
die Tür	door

Culture: German Idioms Part I

Idioms are common expressions that are specific to a language and culture. These expressions are sometimes difficult for people learning a new language because many of them are not supposed to be taken literally.

For example, if you tell another native-English speaker that they have 'hit the nail on the head', both of you will probably know what you are talking about. If you used this same idiom with a native German speaker who is learning English, they might be confused that you are complementing their carpentry skills.

In the same vein, if somebody told you "don't speak through the flowers" in English, you probably wouldn't have a clue what they mean. If, however, you say the same thing German "Sprechen Sie nicht durch die Blumen", they will understand that you mean something like "don't beat around the bush."

Some idioms are similar to ones used in English while others have no counterpart. Using idioms will help you sound more like a native and add some variety to your speech. If you hear a phrase that you don't understand, just ask.

The following are some idioms you might hear

among German speakers. The literal translation is first, followed by a figurative translation if one is necessary:

Den Nagel auf den Kopf treffen/to hit the nail on the head

Da bin ich überfragt./I have been over-asked (It is too much for me)

Der/Die hat nicht alle Tassen im Schrank./He/she doesn't have all the cups in the cupboard.

Kein Aber!/No buts!

Hals und Beinbruch!/Break your neck and leg! (Break a leg!)

Das geht mir auf die Nerven. /It gets on my nerves.

Mir raucht der Kopf./My head is smoking. (My head is spinning.)

Das liegt auf der Hand. /That lies in my hand. (That's plain as the nose on my face.)

Fix und fertig sein/(I'm fast and ready.)(I'm exhausted)

Ende gut, alles gut./All's well that ends well.

Das passt wie die Faust aufs Auge./That fits like a fist in the eye. (I need that like a punch in the nose.)

Blau machen/to make blue (to play hooky)

Wo drückt der Schuh?/Where's your shoe pressing? (What's wrong?)

Das ist Schnee von gestern./That is the snow from yesterday. (That's old news.)

Kein Zuckerschlecken/Not a sugar lick. (Not a cakewalk)

Aller Anfang ist schwer./All beginnings are hard.

Ich verstehe nur Bahnhof./I only understand train station. (It's Greek to me.)

Es liegt mir auf der Zunge./It lies on my tongue. (It's on the tip of my tongue.)

Andere Länder, andere Sitten./Other countries, other customs. (When in Rome…)

Alles hat ein Ende, nur die Wurst hat zwei./Everything has an end, only the sausage has two.

Achtung, fertig, los!/Ready, set, go!

Aus den Augen, aus dem Sinn/Out of sight, out of mind.

Die Axt im Haus erspart den Zimmermann./An ax in the house means you don't need a carpenter. (An apple a day keeps the doctor away.)

keinen Bock/null Bock (auf etwas haben)/to have no goat (to not have any desire to do something)

Borgen macht Sorgen/Borrowing brings worry.

Daumen drücken!/Press your thumbs. (Cross your fingers.)

Es ist nicht alles Gold, was glänzt./Not all that glitters is gold.

Vocabulary: The Family

Nouns:

German	English
der Vater	the father
die Mutter	the mother
der Sohn	the son
die Tochter	the daughter
der Bruder	the brother
die Schwester	the sister
der Onkel	the uncle
die Tante	the aunt
der Opa	the grandpa
der Großvater	the grandfather
die Oma	the grandma
die Großmutter	the grandmother
das Kind	the child
das Enkelkind	the grandchild
der Enkel	the grandson
die Enkelin	the granddaughter

die Geschwister	the siblings
die Verwandten	the relatives
der Erwachsene	the adult
der Schwager	the father-in-law
die Schwägerin	the mother-in-law
der Halbbruder	the half brother
die Halbschwester	the half sister
der Schwiegervater	the step father
die Schwiegermutter	the step mother
der Schwiegersohn	the stepson
die Schwiegertochter	the stepdaughter
die Urgroßmutter	the great-grandmother
der Urgroßvater	the great-grandfather
der Neffe	the nephew
die Nichte	the niece
der (Ehe)mann	the husband
die (Ehe)frau	the wife
der Stiefvater	the stepfather
die Stiefmutter	the stepmother

der Stiefbruder	the stepbrother
die Stiefschwester	the stepsister
der Stiefsohn	the stepson
die Stieftochter	the stepdaughter
der Cousin/Vetter	the male cousin
die Cousine/Kusine	the female cousin

Verbs:

German	**English**
besuchen	to visit
lieben	to love
erziehen	to raise
sprechen	to speak
vermissen	to miss
helfen	to help
streiten	to fight
vergeben	to forgive
wohnen	to reside
leben	to live

Unit 15

Grammar: Genitive Case

Genitive case is used a little differently than the other cases, nominative, accusative and dative. Instead of showing you what role a noun is playing in a sentence, the genitive case shows possession. It is not commonly used in some parts of the German-speaking world, but it is good to know wherever you are.

German	English
der Name des Kindes	the child's name
der Bruder des Mannes	the man's brother
eine Halskette der Frau	a woman's necklace
das Haus der Leute	the people's house

Make sure you do not change the wrong article. In the genitive case, the article of the possessive noun changes. (NOT the noun that is being possessed)

Die (for either feminine or plural) changes to der, and der or das change to des and you add an –s or –es (to a one syllable word) to the end of the noun.

German	English
Die Tante ist die Schwester der Mutter.	The aunt is the sister of the mother.
Die Tante ist die Schwester des Onkels.	The aunt is the sister of the uncle.

Der Onkel ist der Mann der Tante.	The uncle is the husband of the aunt.

When using N-stem or weak masculine nouns in the genitive case, you add the –n ending, but do not add the –s or –es, even though they are all masculine nouns.

German

English

German	English
Der Tempel ist das Haus des Herrn.	The temple is the House of the Lord.
Das Auto des Polizisten fährt schnell.	The car of the police officer drives quickly.
Der Glauben des Protestanten ist stark.	The protestant's faith is strong.

Pronunciation: Eszett

A single S in German makes the sound of the English letter Z. When two S's are together, however, they make the sound of the English letter S. Let's consider a few examples.

German	English
das Schloss	the castle
der Fluss	the river
wissen	to know
passen	to fit

A double S is sometimes written as ß, which is called an Eszett. In the past, the Eszett was used for all instances of a double S. Though you will still see it, its use is becoming less common. Now, only use Eszett in two instances: after a long vowel, or after a combination of vowels. (A diphthong or two vowel sounds in a row, or a tripthong, or three vowel sounds in a row).

Here are some examples for after a long vowel:

German	English
der Fuß	the foot
das Maß	the measurement

Spaß   fun

Here are some other examples for after a diphthong, or combination of vowel sounds:

German	English
weiß	white
heiß	hot
dreißig	thirty

Culture: German Idioms Part II

A und O > das A und O (alpha and omega)
the essential requirements, a must (the beginning and the end)

Ach und Krach > mit Ach und Krach

alle Jubeljahre/nur alle Jubeljahre (einmal)
once in a blue moon, very rarely

Aller Anfang ist schwer.
All beginnings are difficult. The first step is always the hardest.

Aller guten Dinge sind drei.
All good things come in threes./ Third times' a charm

Das ist mein Bier!/Das ist nicht dein Bier!
That's my business./(That's/It's) None of your business!

blau machen
to skip work, play hooky, fake illness to avoid work/school

Borgen macht Sorgen
Neither a borrower nor a lender be.

Daumen drücken!
Keep your fingers crossed! (press your thumbs)

"Ich drücke dir die Daumen." (I'll keep my fingers crossed for you.) - "Drücke mir die Daumen!" (Keep your fingers crossed for me!)

dumm (dumb) > **dümmer als die Polizei erlaubt**
   as dumb as it gets, as dumb as they come ("dumber than the police allow")

Eile mit Weile.
Haste makes waste. More haste, less speed. Make haste slowly.

einen Vogel haben
to be nuts/crazy. (to have a bird [in the head])
   Hast du einen Vogel?
   Are you nuts/crazy?

Pech (tar pitch) > **Pech haben**
   have bad luck
Pech > **großes Pech**
   rotten / terrible luck

Examples: "Pech gehabt!" (Tough luck!) "Sein Pech!" (That's his tough luck!)

Pechvogel ("pitch bird") unlucky devil; walking disaster area

Wasser (water) > **jemandem das Wasser nicht reichen können**
   to not be able to hold a candle to someone; not be in the same league as someone.

"Du kannst ihm das Wasser nicht reichen." (You're just not in the same league he is.) -

Vocabulary: Countries and Nationalities

(Note: Even countries that are spelled the same are pronounced differently in German.)

Nouns:

German	English
Deutschland	Germany
die Schweiz	Switzerland
Österreich	Austria
die Vereinigten Staaten	the United States
Spanien	Spain
Italien	Italy
Griechenland	Greece
Portugal	Portugal
Dänemark	Denmark
Niederlande	the Netherlands
Belgien	Belgium
Poland	Poland
Frankreich	France
Norwegen	Norway

Finnland	Finland
Schweden	Sweden
Großbritannien	Great Britain
Russland	Russia
China	China
Japan	Japan
Ägypten	Egypt
Brasilen	Brasil
Indien	India
Mexiko	Mexico
Ukraine	Ukraine
Nordamerika	North America
Südamerika	South America
Afrika	Africa
Asien	Asia
Europa	Europe
Antarktika	Antarctica
Australien	Australia

Verbs:

German	**English**
herkommen	to come from
auswandern	to emigrate
einwandern	to immigrate

Phrases:

German	**English**
Woher kommen Sie?	Where do you come from?
Was ist Ihre Muttersprache?	What is your native language?
Woher kommen Ihre Vorfahren?	Where do your ancestors come from?

Unit 16

Grammar: Two-Way Prepositions

All of the prepositions you have seen so far have only one possibility of how they affect nouns. Some prepositions make nouns accusative, such as durch, für, gegen, ohne, um, entlang.

There are other prepositions make nouns dative: aus, außer, bei, mit, nach, seit, von, zu, gegenüber.

There are even some prepositions that make nouns go into the genitive case: (an)statt, wegen, trotz, and während.

There are no prepositions that put a noun in the nominative case, which is important to remember, so that you can eliminate that as a possibility.

There is another set of prepositions that can make nouns either accusative or dative case depending on what is happening in the sentence. These are called two-way prepositions. Here are the most common ones:

German	English
in	in
an	at, on
auf	upon

hinter	behind
vor	in front of, before
neben	next to
zwischen	between
unter	under
über	over, about

The first option is accusative. When the subject is going into or toward a location using the preposition, then the preposition makes the noun accusative. The subject cannot be staying in one place, but is in motion toward a destination. It answers the question "where is the noun going?"

German	**English**
Er geht in die Schule.	He goes into the school.
Wir gehen in das Kino.	We are going to the movies.
Ich lege das auf den Schreibtisch.	I am laying that on the desk.
Du hängst das Bild an die Wand.	You hang the picture on the wall.

The second option to make the noun dative. When the subject is in a location or going nowhere then the preposition makes nouns dative. It answers the question "where is the noun?" There is no motion or destination involved.

German

English

Sie sitzt in der Schule.

She is sitting in school.

Wir waren in dem Kino.

We were at the movies.

Es liegt auf dem Tisch.

It is lying on the table.

Das Bild hängt an der Wand.

The picture hangs on the wall.

Pronunciation: Borrowed Words

German has borrowed many words from other languages, especially French and English. These borrowed words generally do not follow the normal rules of pronunciation, but sound like the pronunciation of the language from which they were taken.

Letters like V and J are sometimes pronounced like their English counterparts in words borrowed from English. Take a look at a few examples.

German	English
Vase	vase
November	November
Jeans	jeans
Jazz	jazz

Some words borrowed from French use the French nasal vowels that do not exist in either German or English. Some examples are listed in the following chart.

German	English
der Balcon	the balcony
die Chance	the chance

der Cousin   the male cousin

das Abonnement   the subscription

der Luftballon the   balloon

Some words borrowed from French have the letter combination –age. This combination makes the sound AZH. These are usually words with French roots. Here are some examples.

German	English
die Garage	the garage
die Etage	the floor of a building
die Blamage	the embarrassment

Other borrowed words start with G and have the initial ZH sound. Here are some examples.

German	English
das Genie	the genius
das Gelee	the jelly
das Genre	the genre

Another group of words borrowed from English take the English G pronunciation.

German	English
der Manager	the manager

der Teenager   the teenager

Culture: German History

The Franconian Empire (das Fränkische Reich) of Charles the Great or Charlemagne (Karl der Große), broke apart around the year 900 AD. In the years that followed, German speaking tribes like the Franks (Franken), Saxons (Sachsen), Alemanni (Alemannen), and Bavarians (Bayern) grew closer and closer together to one German Kingdom (Reich der Deutschen) and later to the famous Holy Roman Empire (Heiligen Römischen Reich Deutscher Nation).

By then, Germany was comprised of over 300 independently ruled tribes, speaking many different German dialects. Germanic languages became dominant along the Roman borders (Austria, Germany, Netherlands, Belgium and England) but the rest of the Roman provinces adopted Latin (Romance) dialects.

Tribes, such as the Franks (Franken), Saxons (Sachsen), Angles (Angeln) and Goths (Gothen), with their different dialects transformed the Roman Empire into the Europe that we know today. Germanic languages are spoken now through much of the world, represented mainly by English, German, Dutch and many of the Scandinavian languages.

Vocabulary: Priesthood

Nouns:

German	English
das Priestertum	the priesthood
der Diakon	the deacon
der Lehrer	the teacher
der Priester	the priest
der Bischof	the bishop
der Pfahlpräsident	the branch president
der Berater	the counselor
das Kollegium	the quorum
die Taufe	the baptism
die Segnung	the blessing
der Dienst	service
die Versammlung	the meeting
das Amt	the office (not a room)
das Büro	the office (room)
die Vollmacht	the authority
die Kraft	the power

das Öl   the oil

Verbs:

German	English
dienen	to serve
segnen	to bless
unterstützen	to support/sustain
beraten	to counsel
bestätigen	to confirm
taufen	to baptize
ordinieren	to ordain
beraten	to counsel
empfangen	to receive
helfen	to help
retten	to save
weihen	to dedicate

Unit 17

Grammar: Da and Wo Compounds

Prepositions can be used with the interrogative wo + (r) + preposition to form a question. The r is only added when the preposition begins with a vowel. English has these combinations as well, but they have mostly gone out of style. You will only hear words like "therefore", "thereon", and "whereupon" in old-fashioned English texts. These kinds of compounds, however, are alive and well in German.

German	English
womit	with what
wodurch	through what
woraus	out of what
woran	on what
worauf	upon what
worin	in what
woher	from where
wovor	from what

Prepositions can be used with da + (r) to answer to a wo + (r) + preposition question. They are like two interlocking pieces of a jigsaw puzzle. These forms also used to be heard commonly in English and you will still expresions such as "therefore" and "thereon".

German	English
damit	with that
dadurch	through that
daraus	out of that
darauf	upon that
darin	in that
davor	from that

German	English
Womit fährst du?	With what are you riding?
Ich fahre damit.	I am riding with that.
Worauf steht der Computer?	What does the computer stand on?
Er steht darauf.	It stands on that.
Wovor hast du Angst?	What are you afraid of?
Ich habe davor Angst.	I'm afraid of that.

Pronunciation: The Letter D

D is a friendly letter for English speakers. Most of the time, it acts just as it does in English. This is especially true when it is found at the beginning or the middle of a word. Here are some examples with words that demonstrate this:

Words that Start with D:

German	English
der Dom	the cathedral
die Decke	the comforter
das Dach	the roof
dringend	urgent
durch	through
dumm	dumb
das Ding	the thing
dunkel	dark
denken	to think

Words with D in the Middle

German	English
die Feder	the feather
das Leder	the leather
die Seide	the silk
die Kreide	the chalk
leider	unfortunately
die Nadel	the needle
der Laden	the store

The only difference that you will encounter is when D is the last letter of a word. In this case, the D sounds like an English T. Here are some words where this happens.

German	English
der Tod	death
die Hand	the hand
die Wand	the wall
blind	blind
Leid	sorrow
das Bild	the picture

Culture: German School System

The German school system bears some similarities to the American system, but in many ways, it offers much more choice, providing different tracks for people who wish different career paths. The education system varies between the different states, because schooling in Germany is regulated to a large degree on the local level.

Germany and other European countries have a three track school system. Most German children attend Kindergarten, which is a word English has borrowed, from three to about six years old. It is not a single grade level as it is usually spoken of in English, but encompasses what many Americans might see as pre-school. Once children are six, school is mandatory and students attend an Elementary school (Grundschule).

In some regions, English is required to be taken, starting between first and third grade. After elementary school, each student must make a decision where to continue his or her schooling, depending on their eventual career goals.

Each student undergoes standardized tests to give them a better idea what future might be best for them. Depending on their test scores, there are a few options including Hauptschule, Realschule and Gymnasium.

Hauptschule (grades 5-9 in most German states) teaches the same subjects as other kinds of schools, but at a slower pace and usually leads to enrollment in a vocational school and an apprenticeship.

Realschule (grades 5-10 in most German states) leads to a vocational school and an apprenticeship. High-achieving students can switch to the Gymnasium track.

Gymnasium (grades 5 – 13 in most states) prepares students for a university education after they obtain a diploma called an Abitur. Be sure not to confuse this with the English word gymnasium. In German, this type of gymnasium is called a Turnhalle.

In Europe, a much greater emphasis is given to learning other languages. Each European country is much closer to other countries that speak different languages, which makes knowing more than one language a serious advantage.

Some of the second and third foreign language options, besides English, in the more advanced schools are: French, Spanish, ancient Greek, Latin and Italian. Many schools also offer voluntary study groups for learning other languages, and it is much easier to travel to nearby countries where they can practice with native speakers. So, by the time many German students finish their schooling, they can speak three or four languages reasonably well.

German-speaking Europe is home to some of the oldest universities in the world. For example, the University of Heidelberg was founded in 1386 AD at the time of the Holy Roman Empire. In Germany alone, there are over 70 universities. Unlike universities in the United States, most of the tuition is paid by the government, and the universities to not have sports teams. Going to a university is not a requirement for every type of job, but is reserved for those going in to more academic disciplines such as law and medicine.

Other students choose to enter a Fachhochschule, or vocational school, where they can learn a trade such as carpentry, electrical work or plumbing. Many of these students participate in an apprenticeship or Ausbildung, which usually last between a year and a half to three years. These students work under the supervision of a master in their field and prepare themselves to be masters themselves.

Vocabulary: Free time activities

Nouns:

German	English
das Hobby	the hobby
der Fernseher	the television
der Sport	the sport
das Buch	the book
die Zeitung	the newspaper
die Zeitschrift	the magazine
das Brettspiel	the board game
das Kartenspiel	the card game
die Freizeit	the free time
die Party	the party
der Freitzeitpark	the amusement park
das Konzert	the concert
das Lied	the song
die Band	the band
der Chor	the choir
die klassische Musik	the classical music

die populäre Musik	the popular music
die Rockmusik	the rock music
die Oboe	the oboe
die Geige	the violin
die Flöte	the flute
die Trompete	the trumpet
das Klavier	the piano
die Gitarre	the guitar
das Schlagzeug	the drums
das Mikrofon	the microphone
der Sänger	the singer

Verbs:

German	**English**
entspannen	to relax
nähen	to sew
fernsehen	to watch TV
mahlen	to paint
schreiben	to write
schlafen	to sleep

besuchen	to visit
Sport treiben	to play sports
reiten	to ride a horse
Fahrrad fahren	to write a bike
zelten	to camp
wandern	to hike
lesen	to read
zeichnen	to draw
kochen	to cook
backen	to bake
Ski laufen	to ski
Sporttauchen	to scuba dive
Fotos machen	to take pictures
Klavier spielen	to play piano
Gitarre spielen	to play guitar
Musik hören	to listen to music
singen	to sing
Spaß haben	to have fun
tanzen	to dance

harmonieren	to harmonize
klatschen	to clap

Phrases:

German	**English**
Was machst du in deiner Freizeit?	What do you do in your free time?
Was machst du gerne?	What do you like to do?

Unit 18

Grammar: Reflexive Verbs

Reflexive verbs are used when the subject of the sentence is acting on itself such as someone combing his hair or brushing his teeth. You will see verbs like this listed with the word sich in front of them. Pay close attention to which verbs are reflexive, as some verbs that are reflexive in German are not reflexive in English. Here are a few examples to look out for:

German	English
sich entscheiden	to decide
sich erinnern	to remember
sich fragen	to wonder

Reflexive verbs always require a reflexive pronoun to be added to the sentence. This reflexive pronoun usually come directly after the conjugated verb.

There are two types of reflexive pronouns: accusative and dative. These pronouns are similar to other accusative and dative pronouns, with the exception of sich, which replaces many of the forms. Let's first consider the accusative reflexive pronouns.

Accusative Reflexive Pronouns

mich (ich) uns (wir)

dich (du) euch (ihr)

sich (er) sich (sie)

sich (sie) sich (Sie)

sich (es)

Now let's compare the accusative pronouns with the dative ones. Dative reflexive pronouns are identical to the accusative ones with two exceptions.

Dative Reflexive Pronouns

mir (ich) uns (wir)

dir (du) euch (ihr)

sich (er) sich (sie)

sich (sie) sich (Sie)

sich (es)

There is a simple way to determine when you use accusative and when you use dative. Use the accusative form when no direct object is present and the dative form whenever one is present.

Accusative Examples

German

English

Ich wasche mich.	I am cleaning myself.
Ich kämme mich.	I am combing myself.
Er rasiert sich jeden Morgen.	He shaves every morning.

Dative Examples

German

English

Ich putze mir die Zähne.	I am brushing my teeth.
Ich kämme mir die Haare.	I am brushing my hair.
Er rasiert sich das Gesicht.	He shaves his face.

Pronunciation: The Combination CH

The letter combination ch is common in German, though it can be tricky because it makes two different sounds, depending on the letter or letters it follows. Both of these sounds do not have direct equivalents in English, and so learning them will take some practice.

When ch is found after a, o, u, or au, which are sounds pronounced in the back of the mouth, it is pronounced as a hard ch. This is a grating sound made in the back of the throat that does not have an equivalent in English. Let's take a look at some examples.

German	English
das Loch	the hole
das Buch	the book
der Bauch	the stomach
das Tuch	the towel
der Koch	the cook
der Bach	the stream

When ch is found after e, ä, i, ei, eu, äu, ö, which are vowels pronounced in the front of the mouth, or a consonant, it is pronounced with a soft ch. This sound is made towards the front of the mouth. It resembles the first sound in the English word huge. Here are a few examples.

German	English
ich	I
möchte	would like
Bücher	books
stechen	to sting
gleich	the same
euch	you all
die Sträucher	the bushes

Culture: Architecture in German-Speaking Countries

As you travel around in German-speaking contries, you will doubtless encounter many impressive buildings from old houses, to churches, to soaring castles and cathedrals.

Being in the center of the Europe, German-speaking countries have been influenced by every major architectural movement from the classical Roman styles to the modern age. Styles include Carolingian, Romanesque, Gothic, Renaissance, Baroque, Classical, and Modern. Many of these types of architecture are featured on the different denominations of Euro bills. The smaller bills feature the more historical styles, while the larger bills show the more recent styles.

One thing to remember about Germany in particular, is that many old buildings were completely destroyed as a result of World War I and World War II, and the many bombing raids on German cities. Some cities, such as Frankfurt and Dresden, were hit especially hard and had to be rebuilt. In such cities, the architecture is more modern. Other cities were not affected as much by the war and thus maintain their historical styles.

Some buildings, such as the Gedächtniskirche in Berlin, were left in their damaged state as memorials to those who perished in the war.

In fact, Frankfrut am Main is the only German city to have skyscrapers like you would see in New York City, though other German cities have large buildings.

The oldest city in Germany is Trier, which still contains many examples of Roman architecture, including the Porta Nigra, which is well-preserved ancient Roman city gate.

There are many cathedrals spred through the German-speaking world, and they vary greatly in architectural style. For example, the Cathedral in Speyer is Romanesque, while the Catherdal in Köln is mostly Gothic. It took over 600 years to build and was the tallest structure in the world for a time.

Many of these cathedrals took hundreds of years to build and so are a combination of multiple styles as tastes changed over the centuries. You may even see catherals where one spire looks completely different than another because they were built in vastly different time periods.

There are also a variety of castles, fortresses and palaces still standing throughout the German-speaking world. Some notable castles include medival style castles like Braunfels, the whimsical Neuschwanstein, which is meant to look medival, but isn't, the renessance-style castle in Heidelberg, and Burg Eltz, which is one of the few casltes that has never been destroyed and is still lived in by the same family as it was anciently.

Many European houses are built in a style known as Fachwerk, with a network of visible wood timbers on the outside of the house. The strange thing about Europe is that you often see these old-fashioned buildings right next to modern buildings.

Vocabulary: Adjectives

German	English
groß	tall
kurz	short (height)
klein	short
nett	nice
gemein	mean
dick	thick
dünn	thin
blau	blue
orange	orange
weiß	white
grün	green
schwarz	black
rot	red
braun	brown
lila	pink
heiß	hot
kalt	cold

warm	warm
schnell	fast
langsam	slow
interresant	interesting
langweilig	boring
klug	smart
dumm	dumb
gut	good
schlecht	bad
geduldig	patient
ungeduldig	impatient
blond	blond
rothaarig	red-haired
müde	tired
hübsch	pretty
hässlich	ugly
lustig	funny
nervös	nervous
faul	lazy

künstlerisch	artistic
schön	beautiful
schwach	weak
stark	strong
nett	nice
glücklich	happy
traurig	sad
krank	sick
reich	rich
arm	poor
egoistisch	selfish
selbstsicher	confident
schüchtern	shy
großzügig	generous
ehrlich	honest
verwirrt	confused

Unit 19

Grammar: Relative Clauses

Relative clauses are entire clauses, which describe a noun, known as a antecedent. They are very common in English.

That's the man whom I know very well.

The restaurant, at which we ate last night, was very good.

Siemens, a company based in Germany, produces technology.

In German, relative clauses start with a relative pronoun and are set off by commas. The relative pronouns are as follows. Notice that they are very close to regular pronouns.

	M	F	N	P
Nom	der	die	das	die
Acc	den	die	das	die
Dat	dem	der	dem	denen

Here are some nominative case examples.

German

Ist das der Arzt, der dir geholfen hat?

Ich suche ein Buch, das spannend ist.

Er isst das Fleisch, das am frischsten ist.

Wir sehen die Stiefel, die meine Mutter möchte.

English

Is that the doctor who helped you you?

I'm looking for a book that is suspenseful.

He is eating the meat that is the freshest.

We see the boots that my mother would like.

Here are some accusative case examples.

German

Ich suche einen Wagen, den ich mir leisten kann.

Sind das die Nudeln, die du gekocht hast?

Wo ist das Buch, das Sie mir gegeben haben?

Sie sind die Verwandten, die ich besonders gern sehe.

English

I am looking for a car that I can afford.

Are those the noodles you cooked?

Where is the book that you gave me?

They are the relatives that I especially like to see.

Here are some dative case examples.

German

Er ist ein Untersucher, dem ich gerne helfe.

Es ist das Kind, dem du danken sollst.

Die Leute, bei denen ich wohne, sind sehr nett.

English

He is an investegator whom I gladly help.

He is the child whom you should thank.

The people I live with are very nice.

Pronunciation: Final –E vs. Final –ER

In English, when the letter E is the last letter in a word, it is often silent. Examples include cake, invite, base, among many others.

In German, the letter E is never silent. When it is the final letter of a word, it makes what is called a "schwa" sound, or "uh". This sound is never accented.

Here are some examples of words with E as the last letter.

German	English
die Blume	the flower
die Ente	the duck
die Lampe	die lamp
der Käse	the cheese
die Wolke	the cloud

German has a similar sound that is written –er. In this case, the R is not prounced in the normal way, but it produces an unstressed syllable much like a –e. The sound is slightly different, which is something that you will need to listen for in native German speakers.

German	English
der Vater	the father
die Mutter	the mother
der Bruder	the brother
die Schwester	the sister

Culture: German Regional Accents

Most people don't know that German is one of the most spoken languages in the world; about 120 million people in the world speak German. Among others, German is spoken in Germany, Austria, Switzerland, Belgium, Luxembourg, and Liechtenstein.

For this reason, there are naturally many different German dialects.

You do not only find dialects, however, only in other countries, but rather also in Germany itself. The eastern part of Germany, for example, the Saxon dialect is predominately spoken. In western part of Germany on the other hand, official 'high German' is more often spoken.

Most of the time, the individual words are simply pronounced a bit differently, though often different dialects also have words that are completely their own. For example, in eastern Germany, you would say Huddelei, instead of saying Problem, Ährborn, instead of Kartoffel and Behbe instead of Kuchen.

To tell the truth, every city and even every village in Germany has its own dialect and it is fun to hear these dialects in different parts of the country.

In the same way that you can tell from a person's

dialect in America whether they came from the north or the south, you can quickly tell by a person's dialect whether you are talking to someone from Bavaria, Swabia, or Switzerland.

The dialect that is spoken in Switzerland is called "Schweizerdeutsch". This dialect has different grammar and pronunciation from normal High German. High German is often only used in written form in Switzerland and so it is often called Script German.

One of the biggest differences is the 'ch' sound. In High German, this sound is spoken soft but in Swiss German, it is a hard sound made in the throat of the speaker. The 'ch' sound is used much more often in Swiss German, because, for example, the 'k" sound is said as a 'ch' sound.

Two other large differences are the sounds 'au' and 'ung'. 'Au' as in the words 'Haus' oder "Haut' becomes 'Hut' und 'Hus' in Swiss German. On the other hand 'ung'

There many differences between High German and Swiss German. In High German, consonants on the end of words are sometimes pronounced differently. In Swiss German, it does not happen. For example,in High German, you say 'der Tag' (der Tak), but in Swiss German, you simply say 'der Tag' (der Tag).

In Swiss German, the letter N is left off at the end of some words. From the

words machen and Garten, you get 'mache' and 'Garte'. Normally, you don't use the genitive case, but instead you use the word 'von' to show possession. In German, you would say 'das Buch des Lehrers' but in Swiss German, you say 'das Buch von dem Lehrer'.

Both French and Italian are also common in Switzerland, so you might hear people combining words from different languages. Many common Swiss-German words show influences from French and Italian.

Here are some additional words that differ between Swiss German and the German spoken in Germany:

Germany German	Swiss German	English
das Eis	das Glace	ice cream
das Bisschen	das Bizzeli	a little bit
weinen	brüele	to cry
das Baby	das Buschi	the baby
die Katze	die Busle	the cat
der Käse	der Chäs	the cheese

der Freitag	der Friitig	the Friday
der Grossvater	der Grosspapi	the grandpa
die Sonne	die Sunne	the son
das Fahrrad	das Velo	bicycle

Austrian German even has its own dictionary. The German in Austria is not

so different as German in the Switzerland, but there are still differences.

Some vocabulary is different, In Germany, you say "Fußgänger" and in

Austria, you normally say "Fußgeher". Instead of saying "Januar", there you

say "Jänner" and instead of "dieses Jahr", you say "heuer". Instead of

"Kartoffel" you say "Erdäpfel" and instead of "Schrank", "Kasten".

Grammar is also a bit different. Some verbs that use "haben" as a helping

verb, instead use sein. For example, you say "ich bin gessessen" instead of

"ich habe gesessen". You also use the simple past form only rarely.

Here are some additional words that differ between Austrian German and the German spoken in Germany:

Germany German	Austrian German	English
am Morgen	in der Früh	in the morning
der Becher	das Häferl	the cup
das Bonbon	das Zuckerl	the candy
das Brötchen	die Semmel	the roll
das Büro	die Kanzlei	the office
der Februar	der Feber	February
das Hackfleisch	das Faschierte	ground meat
das Krankenhaus	das Spital	hospital
die Tomate	der Paradeiser	tomato
das T-Shirt	das Leibchen	T-shirt
der Umschlag	das Kuvert	envelope

Vocabulary: Body

Nouns:

German	English
der Arm	the arm
der Rücken	the back
das Blut	the blood
das Gehirn	the brain
die Brust	the chest
das Ohr	the ear
das Auge	the eye
das Gesicht	the face
der Fingernagel	the fingernail
der Zehnagel	the toenail
der Fuß	the foot
die Stirn	the forehead
das Haar	the hair
der Hals	the throat
die Hand	the hand
der Kopf	the head

das Herz	the heart
das Knie	the knee
das Bein	the leg
die Lippen	the lips
der Mund	the mouth
der Nacken	the neck
die Nase	the nose
die Schulter	the shoulder
die Haut	the skin
der Körper	the body
der Bauch	the stomach
die Zähne	the teeth
die Zunge	the tongue
die Wimpern	the eyelashes
die Augenbrauen	the eyebrows
der Ellbogen	the elbow
der Knöchel	the ankle
die Hüfte	the hip
das Handgelenk	the wrist

der Muskel	the muscle
der Daumen	the thumb
der Finger	the finger
das Gesicht	the face
der Krankenwagen	the ambulance
der gebrochene Knochen	the broken bone
die Klinik	the clinic
der Arzt/die Ärztin	the doctor
die Krankenschwester	the female nurse
der Krankenpfleger	the male nurse
die Medizin	the medicine
der Patient	the patient
das Rezept	the prescription
die Magenschmerzen	the stomachache
die Kopfschmerzen	the headache
der Husten	the cough
die Erkältung	the cold
der Feber	the fever
die Grippe	the flu

der Krebs	the cancer
der Diabetes	the diabetes
der Ohrenschmerz	the earache
das Asthma	the asthma
der Herzinfarkt	the heart attack
die Narbe	the scar
der Umfall	the accident
die Narbe	the scar
die Spritze	the injection
die Diagnose	the diagnosis

Adjectives

German	English
gesund	healthy
krank	sick
stark	strong
schwach	weak
rau	hoarse
ansteckend	contagious

in guter Form	in good shape
in schlechter Form	in bad shape
sterbenskrank	seriously ill

Verbs

German	English
sich bewegen	to move
sich verletzen	to injure
krank werden	to become sick
Fieber haben	to have a fever
sich nicht wohl fühlen	to not feel good
Medikamente nehmen	to take medicine
sich übergeben	to throw up
sich ausruhen	to relax
zunehmen	to gain weight
abnehmen	to lose weight
husten	to cough
niesen	to sneeze
anschwellen	to swell
riechen	to smell

schmecken	to taste
sehen	to see
fühlen	to feel
hören	to hear
sitzen	to sit
stehen	to stand

Unit 20

Grammar: Als, wenn, wann

In German, you need to make sure you use the correct one of three words: als, wenn, and wann The one that you use will depend on the context of the sentence.

Use als when talking about past events, such as talking about things you did when you were young. Here are a few examples to demonstrate this:

German

Als ich jünger war, hatte ich Angst vor Schlangen.

Als ich Kind war, musste ich eine Brille tragen.

Als er vorbeikam, war ich nicht dort.

English

When I was younger, I was scared of snakes.

When I was a kid, I had to wear glasses.

When he came by, I was not there.

Wann is another mix-up word because it also means *when*, but only when you are asking a question. Even though both wann and wenn sound like the English word when, never use wenn when posing a question. Here are some examples of using this word.

German	English
Wann kommt der Bus?	When is the bus coming?
Wann haben Sie Zeit?	When do you have time?
Wann fängt die Kirche an?	When does church start?

Wenn means *whenever* or *if*. Just remember never to use it in the past tense or when posing a question. Pay attention to the meaning of the following sentences.

German

Wenn er Hunger hat, isst er.

Wenn das Buch wahr ist, komme ich zur Kirche.

Wenn ich bete, fühle ich mich besser.

English

When(ever) he is hungry, he eats.

When the book is true, I'll come to church.

When(ever) I pray, I feel better.

Another word you need to learn is **ob**, which can also mean if. You only use it, however, when you could substitute the word whether for if and have it still make sense. Here are a few examples of this.

German

Ich weiß nicht, ob sie kommt.

Wissen Sie ob wir laufen oder fahren?

Wie weiß man, ob das Evangelium war ist?

English

I don't know if she is coming.

Do you know if we are walking or driving?

How does one know if the gospel is true?

Pronunciation: M and N

Both M and N are letters in German that should not give you too much trouble. Most of the time, they will sound exactly like they do in English. Here are some examples of German words that include M and N.

Words with M in the Beginning:

German	English
die Macht	the power
der Mann	the man
der Magen	the stomach
der Mensch	the person
der Missionar	the missionary
der Mormone	the Mormon
der Mönch	the monk

Words with N in the Beginning:

German	English
die Nacht	the night
die Nichte	the niece
der Neffe	the nephew

der Nebel	the fog
der Nachbar	the neighbor
die Nonne	the nun

There are just a few things to remember, especially with the letter N. The first thing is that you will sometimes see the letter N with other consonnants, and these combinations will sound different than they do in English.

For example, in English, the first letter is silent when you have the combinations KN, as in the word *knight* or *knife*, or the combination GN as in the word gnome. In German, however, both letters are fully pronounced, one after the other. Here are some examples of German words where this happens:

Words with KN

German	English
der Knecht	the servant
die Knospe	the bud
der Knabe	the boy

Words with GN

German	English
der Gnom	the gnome
die Gnade	the grace
gnädig	merciful

You will also see that when –EN is at the end of a German word, it actually sounds like –M. The most common example of this is the **haben**, which you will often hear as **habem**.

Culture: Famous German Speakers

The following are famous German speakers who are not musicians, artists, or fiction authors. You will likely see streets named after some of these figures in cities in German-speaking countries.

Karl Marx

Lived: 1818-1883

Bio: Karl Max was a notable German philosopher and economist. His most important work was the Communist Manifesto, which outlined the principles of a communist government. He worked with another revolutionary named Friedrich Engels to speak against capitalism and for communism as the fairest form of government. Many governments such as East Germany, the U.S.S.R. and China based their governments on Marxist philosophies.

Friedrich Bayer

Lived: 1825-1880

Bio: Friedrich Bayer was born in Wuppertal Germany and went on to found the Bayer Company, which continues to this day as a major provider of chemical and pharmaceutical products.

Rudolf Diesel

Lived: 1858-1913

Bio: Many of the world's most famous car makers got their start in Germany. Some of them started famous car brands such as BMW (Franz Josef Popp), Mercedes Benz (Karl Benz), Audi (August Horch), Daimler-Chrysler (Gottlieb Daimler), or Porsche (Ferdinand Porsche).

A mechanical engineer named Rudolf Diesel made one of the most significant contributions to the automotive world as the inventor of the Diesel engine, which is still used in many trucks and other large vehicles today.

Oscar Ferdinand Mayer

Lived: (1859-1955)

Bio: Oscar was born in Germay, and emigrated to Detroit while a teenager. He later moved to Chicago, and started a butcher shop of his own. His company grew steadily into the Oscar Mayer company, which is now a popular processed-meat company.

Henry E. Steinway (Steinweg)

Lived: 1791-1871

Bio: Henry was born in what is now Germany and survived a tragic childhood that left him an orphan at 15. He fought in the war against Napoleon and then took work first as a carpenter and then as an apprentice to an organ builder. He discovered there his passion for music and took over as the organist for the church. He took to building his own instruments from small ones such as guitars, gradualling building up to pianos.

In 1850, Henry moved to New York City and

changed his name from Steinweg to Steinway. He founded his own instrument company in 1853 with his five sons called Steinway and Sons. Their pianos won many awards and the company is now builds a internationaly-respected brand of piano.

Werner von Siemens

Lived: 1816-1892

Bio: Werner grew up on a farm as one of fourteen children, and grew up to be a famous German inventor and businessman. His name has been adopted as a measurement of electrical conductance (how easily electricity can flow through a substance). The measurement is abbreviated as SI. In addition, he founded the Siemens Company, which has grown into a large electrical and telecommunications company.

Adolf and Rudolf Dassler

Lived: 1900-1978

Bio: Adolf was born in Germany, and often went by the name "Adi". He trained as a cobbler, and started to make his own sports shoes with his brother, Rudolf, after returning military service in World War I. Their business, die Gebrüder Dassler Schuhfabrik, took off, and they became a suppier of shoes for many atheletes of the 1928 and 1936 Olympic games. During the 1936 Summer Olympics in Beriln, Jesse Owens from the United States wore Adi's shoes and won four gold medals.

After World War II, Adi and Rudolf parted ways and founded separate companies. Rudolf founded a company called Puma, (originally called Ruda) while Adi founded Adidas, a combination of his nickname and part of his last name. Both companies flourished and still produce athletic clothing and shoes in many countries.

Otto von Bismarck

Lived: (1815-1898)

Bio: Otto is one of the most important figures in modern German politics. He was born to a noble father and commoner mother, and started to study for a law degree at the age of 17. He was elected to the Prussian parliament in 1849. Prussia was a large German-speaking kingdom that was only one of many small kingdoms that make up what is now Germany.

Otto worked to bring these kingdoms that shared a

common language and heritage together into a single German kingdom. On Jan 18th, 1871, Otto was crowned the first Royal Chancelor of Germany in the Hall of Mirrors in the palace at Versailles. The new kingdom enjoyed peace until the outbreak of World War I in 1914.

Nicolaus Copernicus

Lived: 1473-1543

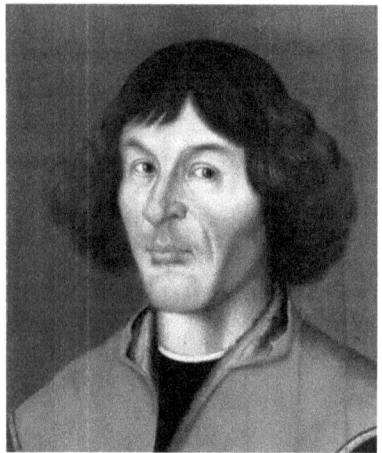

Bio:

Nicolaus was an astronomer who lived during the Renaissance period. He was the first astronomer to propose a model of the universe based on having the sun at the center of the universe instead of the earth. He published an important work on astronomy called "On the Revelutions of Celestial Spheres", which is often seen as the starting point of modern astronomy. He wrote mostly in Latin, though was said to have also spoke German, Polish, Greek and Italian.

Albert Einstein

Lived: 1879-1955

Bio: Albert Einstein was a German scientist and professor, whose name is now associated with the word 'genius'. He was born in 1879 in Ulm, Germany. Among many other scientific achievements, he developed the famous Theory of Relativity (E=MC2) and won the Noble Prize in Physics for it in the year 1921. Again, this is not correct. He won the Noble prize for his work on the Photoelectric effect, that light is a particle as well as a wave.

He was known all over the world. During his life, he lived in Germany, Switzerland, Italy, but he finally moved to the United States in 1933 and became a US citizen. There, he became a professor in Princeton, New Jersey. His decision to leave Germany came about, because Adolf Hitler had seized power at that time and Einstein disagreed with his policies, and feared for his own safety because of his jewish heritage.

Thanks to his theories, we have the television, the laser, the DVD player, among others. He also helped discover nuclear fission and this led to the construction of the atom bomb (theManhattan Project). Although he helped with this project, he was completely against war and did not want people to die because of his research.

Einstein is stil prevalent in popular culture as the epitome of the absent minded professor or the brilliant scientist with unruly hair. He died at 76 years of age, but left a powerful legacy for scientists to build on.

Daniel Gabriel Fahrenheit

Lived: 1686-1736

Bio:

Daniel was a German engineer, scientist and glass blower who is best known for inventing the mercury thermometer and the system of the measuring temperature that was named after him. Until Europe adopted the Celsius scale, Fahrenheit's scale was widely used. It is still used in the United States.

Johannes Gutenberg

Lived: 1398-1468

Bio:

Johannes Gutenberg was born in Mainz, Germany and became a printer and publisher. He was the first European who used the 'mechanical movable type printing and was the inventor of the printing press.

Because of his achievements, Gutenberg is known as the Father of the "German Printing Revolution". Gutenberg's printing technology spread throughout Europe and later all around the world. His major work, the famous Gutenberg Bible (Gutenberg Bibel) is one of the most beautifully crafted bibles with many illustrations and incredible print quality for its time. It was the first version of the Bible to be mass produced, though the print run was only 180 copies. This trend allowed many people access to the Bible who had never been able to read it before.

Gutenberg's inventions influenced other important matters, such as the printing and distribution of the Luther Bible and other important documents. The greater availability of God's word influenced many of the major figures of the Reformation.

Wilhelm Conrad Röntgen

Lived: 1845 - 1923

Bio: Wilhelm was a German physicist who is most well known for producing and detecting electromagnetic radiation, which led to the development of X-rays, also known as Röntgen rays. He only termed the rays X-rays as a placeholder, because X is used to designate an unknown in math. English still uses X-rays, but many other languages, including German, still use a form of Röntgen's name. This accomplishment earned in the Nobel Prize in Physics in 1901. He even has a radioactive element on the periodic table named after him, element 111, Roentgenium.

Martin Luther

Lived: 1483-1546

Bio:

Martin Luther was born in Eisleben, Germany on November 10th, 1483 and was a catholic priest, a professor of theology and became the 'father' of the protestant church. In German, when people speak say they are Evangelisch, it means that they are Lutheran. Besides the Catholic Church, the Lutheran Church is one of the official churches recognized by the German State.

As a young man, Martin had a near death experience in a thunderstorm cired out for help, promising that he would become a monk if his life was spared. He left law school and made good on his promise, against the wishes of his family and friends.

In his new life as a monk, Luther noticed practices in the Catholic Church with which he did not agree. He is famous for his 95 theses or points he sent to the bishop of Mainz as a scholarly objection to some of the churches' practices such as asking people for money in order for them to be forgiven of sins.

These thesis and Luther's objections eventually led to his excommunication from the Catholic Church and his condemnation as an outlaw by Holy Roman Emperor Charles V. Luther was given refuge at Wartburg Castle, close to Eisenach, Germany. It was here that he translated the New Testament from ancient Greek into German and wrote several religious essays.

His objective in translating the bible was to make it more accessible to the people. He wrote worship services in German, instead of Latin, to educate and help the people to understand important doctrines. Because of his masterful bible translation and sermons, using Mitteldeutsch which was understood by a broad variety of Germans, Luther was influential for the spread of the written German language.

His influence and that of other religious reformers caused many people to break from the Catholic Church, which led to a complete unheaval of life in Europe, and eventually led to armed conflicts such as the 30 Year's War. To this day, different regions of the German-speaking countries remain either predominantly Lutheran or Catholic.

Martin Luther organized the Protestant Church in 1526 and wrote numerous hymns, also in German instead of Latin. One of his most well-known hymns is, A Mighty Fortress Is Our God (Ein feste Burg ist unser Gott).

Albert Schweitzer

Lived: 1875-1965

Bio: Albert was a German and French philosopher and theologian. He won the Nobel Peace Prize in 1952 for his humanitarian work, epsically for founding the Albert Schweitzer Hospital in what is now Gabon, Africa. He was also an accomplished organist with a passion for the music of Johann Sebastian Bach. He not only played well, but worked to preserve old pipe organs.

Franz Ferdinand

Lived: 1863 - 1914

Bio: Franz Feridnand was the Archduke of the Austro-Hungarian Empire and the heir to the throne. His greatest significance came with his death, an assaination that led Austria-Hungary to declare war on Serbia. This drew other nations into the fray, starting World War I. He and his wife were shot while riding in an open car through Sarajevo, the capital of Bosnia/Herzegovina by a 19 old assassin.

Sigmund Freud

Lived: 1856 - 1939

Bio: Sigmund was an Austrian neurologist who developed many theories about human development, including the new field of psychoanalysis. His work on the subconscious and other areas of the human mind continue to influence many neurologists today.

Freud is also still alive in popular culture. When you say misspeak, and what you said could reveal hidden intentions, you are said to have commited a "Freudian Slip".

Oskar Schindler

Lived: 1908 – 1974

Bio: Oskar was born in what was then the Austria-Hungarian empire. He is best known for saving over 1,100 Jews from death at the hands of the Nazis by employing them in his factories in modern-day Poland and the Czech Republic. His life has been the subject of famous books and movies such as "Schindler's List".

Georg Johannes von Trapp

Lived: 1880 - 1947

Bio: Georg was a naval officer for the Austro-Hungarian Empire. The story of his family was the inspiration for the popular stage musical and movie, The Sound of Music. Though many of the events depecticted in the Sound of Music mirror historical events, the playrights, the famous pair Rogers and Hammerstein, took liberties with the plot. All of the names and ages of the children have been changed, as well as some details of their flight from Austria.

During the First World War, he earned many commendations. After the war, the Austro-Hungarian Empire collapsed into the general borders that is has today. This left the country without a coastline and so no use for a navy, and thus no use for Georg's services.

His first wife, Agathe Whitehead bore him many children, but died early of scarlet fever. The family moved to a town near Salzburg, Austria. Georg hired a tutor for one of his sick children. He married this woman, Maria Kuschera, and has a few more children with her.

After losing their family fortune in a failed bank, the Von Trapps turned their hobby of singing into a profession to raise money. Fearing the Nazi movement and its consequences, Georg took his family by train first to Italy and then settled in the United States.

Henri Nestle

Lived: 1814-1890

Bio: Henri was a German confectioner who founded
Nestle, which is now the world's largest food and
beverage company. He was born in Frankfurt
Germany as the eleventh of forteen children, and
the business was always a family one. In the dialect
of his family, "Nestle" means "a small bird's nest",
which can be seen on the company logo.

Huldrych Zwingli

Lived: 1484 - 1531

Bio: Hyldrych was a leader of the Reformation in Switzerland. As a pastor, he spoke out about ideas to reform the Catholic Church such as fasting during Lent, corruption in Church leadership, not allowing priests to marry and using images in places of worship. Eventually, he introduced an alternative church service to replace the traditional Catholic mass.

His ideas spread throughout Switzerland, and causes divisions between the different provinces of Switzerland. These conflicts escalated into deadly attacks, and Hyldrch lost his life during an attack on Zurich. Though he did not completely agree with Martin Luther, the two men shared the same goal of reforming the Catholic Church and faced fierce opposition.

Vocabulary: The City

Nouns:

German	English
das Rathaus	the city hall
das Krankenhaus	the hospital
die Post	the post office
die Schule	the school
die Feuerwache	the fire station
die Straße	the street
der Bahnhof	the train station
der Hauptbahnhof	the main trainstation
die Bushaltestelle	the bus stop
der Laden	the shop
das Einkaufszentrum	the mall/shopping center
das Kaufhaus	the department store
das Restaurant	the restaurant
der Supermarkt	the supermarket
der Parkplatz	the parking lot
die Polizeiwache	the police station

das Museum	the museum
das Denkmal	the memorial
die Kirche	the church
der Stadtteil	the city district
das Dorf	the village
die Hauptstadt	the capital city
die Bushaltestelle	the bus stop
die Ubahn	the subway
die Ampel	the traffic signal

Verbs:

German	English
einkaufen	to buy
laufen	to walk
fahren	to drive
suchen	to seek
Fahrrad fahren	to ride a bicycle
bummeln	to wander around
besichtigen	to tour something

spazieren	to go on a walk
einsteigen	to board
aussteigen	to disembark

Phrases:

German	English
German	**English**
Wo findet man…	Where does one find…
Welche Buslinie…	Which bus line…
Wo ist die Bushallestelle?	Where is the bus stop?

Unit 21

Grammar: Passive Voice

Active voice is when the subject of the sentence performs the action. The passive voice occurs when the subject is not directly doing the action in the sentence.

Most of the time, it is best to use the active voice, but the passive voice does have its uses, and is especially popular on public German signs. Passive sentances are usually longer and less to the point. Take a look at the difference between an active and a passive sentence

Active: I wrote the book.

Passive: The book was written by me.

Instead of using the word by when making passive sentances, German forms the passive voice uses a form of the verb **werden** and a past participle. If the subject is present, it is paired with the word **von** or **durch**, which puts it in the dative case.

Active: Ich schrieb das Buch or Ich habe das Buch geschrieben.

Passive: Das Buch wurde von mir geschrieben.

The sentence takes on a slightly different meaning depending on the tense of the word **werden**. Take a

look at the following examples.

Present

German	English
Die Kekse werden von uns gegessen.	The cookies are being eaten by us.
Das Lied wird von ihm gesungen.	The song is being sung by him.

Present   Perfect

German	English
Die Kekse sind von uns gegessen worden.	The cookies were eaten by us.
Das Lied ist von ihm gesungen worden.	The song was sung by him.

Simple Past

German	English
Die Kekse wurden von uns gegessen.	The cookies were eaten by us.
Das Lied wurde von ihm gesungen.	The song was sung by him.

Past Perfect

German	English
Die Kekse waren von uns gegessen worden.	The cookies had been eaten by us.
Das Lied war von ihm gesungen worden.	The song had been sung by him.

Future

German	English
Die Kekse werden von uns gegessen werden.	The cookies will be eaten by us.
Das Lied wird von ihm gesungen werden.	The song will be sung by him.

The passive voice is often used to answer the question: Wo wurden Sie geboren? (Where were you born?)

German	English
Ich wurde in Deutschland geboren.	I was born in Germany.

Er wurde in den Vereinigten Staaten geboren.   He was born in the United States.

Pronunciation: GN, NG, and PF

The letter combination NG exists in both English and German. Both languages have the word finger/der Finger, but each if pronounced a little differently.

In English, there is a strong G sound in the second syllable, while German has a much softer G sound. When you see NG in German, you should never pronounce it with a hard G.

Take a look at a few examples.

German	English
der Hunger	the hunger
singen	to sing
der Finger	the finger

The letter combination GN is more common in German than English. In English, the G is usually silent. In German, however, both letters are completely pronounced.

Here are some German words that contain this letter combination.

German	English
der Gnom	the gnome

die Gnade	the grace
gnädig	merciful

The letter combination PF is not widely used in English, but can be found in all locations within a word in German. It is produced as a single sound, with both the P and the F being represented. Here are a variety of examples, with PF occurring in different places in a word.

German	English
der Dampf	the steam
das Pferd	the horse
der Kopf	the head
der Knopf	the button
das Pfund	the pound
der Pfirsich	the peach
der Tropfen	the drop

Culture: German Sports

Many Germans are huge sports fans. Though you will see people playing baseball or basketball, the real passion of Germans is soccer or **Fußball**. Most large German cities have a professional soccer team, and the German national team often fares well in international competitions such as the World Cup.

Sports are a big deal in Germany. From tennis to horseback riding, Gymnastics to Soccer, German's most cherished free time activity is playing on teams and in sport clubs.

Many people join sport organizations and clubs when they are young. With more than 5.5 million members, the German Fußball-Bund (German Soccer Federation or DFB) is the most popular sports organization.

Germany also has a professional soccer league, the Deutsche Bundesliga. German soccer or Fußball is played in thousands of amateur clubs as well. Almost every big city in Germany has its own soccer stadium, which are filled to capacity throughout the soccer season with loyal fans, rooting for their team.

Some of the most famous soccer teams are FC Bayern München, 1.FC Köln, Hamburger SV, Borussia Dortmund, Werder Bremen. Germany has hosted soccer's World Cup many times and is often a good contender every time the World Cup comes around.

When you visit one of the public parks in Germany, you will find many people enjoying a quick game of soccer as well.

Vocabulary: Weather

Nouns:

German	English
die Wolke	the cloud
der Regen	the rain
der Schnee	the snow
der Wind	the wind
die Brise	the breeze
die Flut	the flood
die Sonne	the sun
der Nebel	the fog
das Glatteis	the ice, freezing rain
der Sturm	the storm
der Schneesturm	the blizzard
der Wirbelsturm	the hurricane
der Tornado	the tornado
der Donner	the thunder
der Blitz	the lightning
der Hagel	the hail

das Grad	the degree
der Wetterbericht	the weather report
die Voraussagung	the forecast
das Thermometer	the thermometer
die Flutwelle	the tidal wave

Verbs:

German	English
regnen	to rain
schneien	to snow
fallen	to fall
scheinen	to shine
blasen	to blow
schlagen	to strike
frieren	to freeze
schmelzen	to melt
vorbereiten	to prepare
hoffen	to hope
voraussagen	to forecast
entkommen	to escape

Phrases:

German	**English**
Wie ist das Wetter?	How is the weather?
Was steht im Wetterbericht?	What does the weather report say?
Das Wetter ist gut.	The weather is good.
Das Wetter is schlecht.	The weather is bad.
Mir ist kalt.	It's cold (to me).
Mir ist warm.	It's warm (to me).
Die Sonne scheint.	The sun is shining.
Es ist bewölkt.	It is cloudy.
Es regnet.	It is raining.
Es schneit.	It is snowing.

Unit 22

Grammar: Weak Masculine Nouns

There are a group of nouns that act strangely when compared to other nouns. All of these nouns are masculine (words that take *der* as an article) and all change in the same way, by adding –en or –n on the end whenever they are used as anything but the subject. (nominative case)

The good thing about these nouns is that they are not too hard to spot once you know what to look for. Most of them are either male professions or animals, which makes them easy to remember. There are also certain endings that will help you spot a weak masculine noun. Here are some of those endings and an example German word with each ending.

-ant   der Protestant

-arch   der Patriarch

-ent   der Student

-ist   der Buddist

-oge   der Anthropologe

-om   der Astronom

-oph   der Philosoph

-ot   der Pilot

Pronunciation: CK and CHS

The letter combination CHS is pronounced like the English letter combination KS, which is the same sound heard in the word oxen. Here are some examples of German words that contain this sound.

German	*English*
sechs	six
wachsen	to grow
die Achsel	the armpit

The combination CK in German, is always pronounced like an English K. The vowel before it is always short. Be careful not to mix it up with CH. Take a look at some examples.

German	English
der Scheck	the check
der Stock	the stick
das Glück	the happiness

Culture: German Art

Albrecht Dürer

Lived: 1471-1528

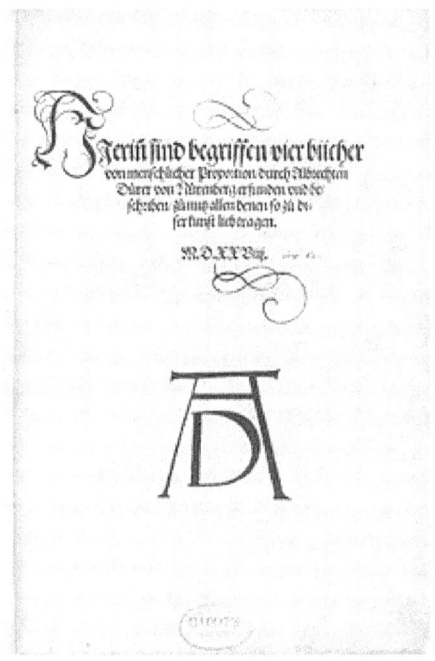

Bio: Albrecht Dürer was one of the most famous German artists of all time. He worked both as a painter and engraver and many of his works appear in churches and have religious themes, such as biblical scenes. He is also known for his portraits, both of himself and other notables.

Albrecht was the son of the goldsmith in a large family of more than fourteen children. He spent years wandering through different cities, learning from a variety of other artistic masters. He spent much of his time in Italy, which time would heavily influence his artistic style.

When looking at a work from Dürer, look for his monogram signature: a large block A with a D inside.

Famous Works: Knight, Death and the Devi, Saint

Jerome in his Study, Dürer's Rhinoceros, Melencolia I, Praying Hands, The Adoration of the Magi

Matthias Grünewald

Lived: 1470-1528

Bio:

Matthias was a painter during the German Renaissance who focused on religious works. Most of his paintings were lost in a shipwreck, and so only ten of his paintings have survived. Like Albrecht Dürer, Matthias used a monogram symbol to sign his works.

Famous Works: Isenheim Altarpiece

Hans Holbein the Elder, Hans Holbein the Younger

Lived: 1460-1524, 1497-1543)

Bio: Hans Holbein and his son were both German painters who painted Gothic religious paintings, woodcuts and windows. Hans Holbein the Younger worked as the royal painter to King Henry VIII, which included painting portraits and designing other decorations.

Famous Works: The Triumphs of Caesar, Portrait of Sir Thomas More, The Ambassadors, Portrait of King Henry VIII

Albrecht Altdorfer:

Lived: 1480 - 1538

Bio:

Albrecht was a Renaissance painter, engraver and architect. He was part of a movement called the Danube School, after the Danube River, whose artists set biblical scenes and other historical subjects against lush landscape backgrounds. He was also known for making small and intricate engravings.

Famous Works: Resurrection, The Battle of Issus/Alexander

Caspar David Friedrich

Lived: 1774-1840

Bio: Caspar was a Romantic painter who specialized in landscapes. Many of his paintings have allegorical meanings, incoperating human figures, landscapes, mists and ruins. Instead of focusing on capturing reality exactly, his works focused on a subject's emotional response to a scene. Caspar was born in Sweden, but eventually settled in the German city of Dresden.

Famous Works: Wanderer above the Sea of Fog, Chalk Cliffs on Rügen, the Abbey in the Oakwood

Heinrich Hofmann

Lived: 1885-1957

Bio: Heinrich was a famous German photographer, best known for his many published fotographs of Adolph Hitler. In 1920, Hitler chose him as his official photographer and the two became close friends. His photographs were used in a variety of settings from magazines to picture boks, and even postage stamps. He received royalties for every time his images were used, even on stamps, which provided him a large income. He was arrested and tried after World War II by Americans and spent four years in prison for Nazi profiteering.

Vocabulary: Animals and Nature

Nouns:

German	English
der Hund	the dog
die Katze	the cat
der Vogel	the bird
der Bär	the bear
das Pferd	the horse
der Löwe	the lion
der Tiger	the tiger
der Elefant	the elephant
das Nilpferd	the hippo
der Frosch	the frog
die Schildkröte	the turtle
der Schwan	the swan
die Ganz	the goose
die Ameise	the ant
der Papagei	the parrot
das Krokodil	the crodile

die Ziege	the goat
das Schaf	the sheep
der Hahn	the rooster
die Henne	the hen
das Schwein	the pig
die Kuh	the cow
die Ente	the duck
das Tier	the animal
das Haustier	the pet
der Zoo	the zoo
die Sonne	the sun
der Mond	the moon
der Stern	the star
der Baum	the tree
der Regenbogen	the rainbow
der Berg	the mountain
die Luft	the air
die Brise	the breeze
der Wasserfall	the waterfall

die Wüste	the desert
die Blume	the flower
das Gras	the grass
das Insekt	the insect
die Ameise	the ant
der Dschungel	the jungle
der See	the lake
der Regen	the rain
der Schmetterling	the butterfly
die Welt	the world
de Erde	the earth
die Wolke	the cloud
der Planet	the plant
die Pflanze	the plant
das Meer	the ocean
der Fluss	the river
das Ufer	the river bank
der Bach	the stream
der Stein	the stone

der Busch	the bush
die Luft	the air
das Flachland	the plain
die Tundra	the tundra
die Wüste	the deseret
der Dschungel	the jungle
der Kreis	the county
das Land	the country
die Grenze	the border
der Staat	the state
der Breitengrad	the latitude
der Längengrad	the longitude
die Bergkette	the mountain range
der Hügel	the hill
das Plateau	the plateau
die Halbinsel	the peninsula
die Insel	the island
der Vulkan	the volcano
der Äquator	the equator

Verbs:

German	English
füttern	to feed animals
fressen	to eat (for animals)
streicheln	to pet
kämmen	to comb
baden	to bathe
spazieren gehen	to go on a walk
rennen	to run
pflegen	to care for
scheinen	to shine
wachsen	to grow
sterben	to die
blühen	to bloom
schätzen	to treasure

Phrases:

German	English
Hast du ein Haustier?	Do you have a pet?

Unit 23

Grammar: Infinities plus zu

Using an infinitive plus the word zu/to works the same in English as it does in German. The infinitive form is put after the word zu at the end of a sentence.

German	English
Er hat keine Zeit zu lesen.	He has no time to read.
Hans versucht zu tanzen.	Hans is trying to dance.
Gibt es etwas zu essen?	Is there something to eat?

If the infinitive is a separable verb, the zu comes between the prefix and the stem.

German	English
Er bittet dich wegzugehen.	He is asking you to go away.
Elke versucht fernzusehen.	Elke is trying to watch TV.
Wir haben kein Geld einzukaufen.	We don't have any money to shop.

There are three prepositions that work with infinitive forms to change the meaning. These are *um, ohne* and *anstatt*. When paired with the *zu* + infinitive construction, they mean "in order to do something", "without doing something", and "instead of doing something". These phrases are always set off by a comma.

Here are some examples with **um**. Notice that in English, you can say the sentence without saying the words in order.

German	English
Ich bin hier, um Deutsch zu lernen.	I am here (in order) to learn German.
Sie kommt zu ihm, um ihm zu helfen.	Sie is coming to him (in order) to help him.
Er ist hier, um den Zahnarzt zu sehen.	He is here (in order) to see the dentist.

Here are some examples with the word **ohne**.

German	English
Er ging, ohne mir die Antwort zu sagen.	He went without telling me the answer.
Sie haben die Kekse gegessen, ohne zu fragen.	They ate the cookies without asking.
Du dienst nicht, ohne viel zu lernen.	You won't serve, without learning a lot.

Here are some examples with the word **anstatt**.

German	English
Sie spricht viel, anstatt zu lernen.	She speaks a lot instead of learning.
Ich gehe zur Schule, anstatt zu essen.	We are going to school instead of eating.
Er spielt, anstatt schlafen.	He is playing instead of sleeping.

Pronunciation: The Letter G

Most of the time, G is not difficult to pronounce. This is because, the letter G in German sounds like its equivalent in English when it appears at the beginning or middle of the word.

G at the Beginning

German	English
gestern	yesterday
die Gabel	the fork
die Gasse	the avenue
gut	good
grün	green

G in the Middle

German	English
der Vogel	the bird
die Fliege	fly
folgen	to follow

Only when a G comes at the end of a word, and is not preceded by the letter I, it makes the sound of the English letter K. The following words are good examples of this.

G at the End

German	English
klug	intelligent
der Sieg	victory
der Zug	the train
der Krieg	the war
der Flug	the flight

When a word ends with the letter combination IG, it makes the sound of a soft CH. This can vary a bit depending on what country or region you are in. Sometimes, you will hear others pronounce this like a K as well.

IG at the End

German	English
richtig	correct
lustig	funny
der Honig	the honey
fertig	finished
der König	the king
vierzig	forty

Culture: German Authors and Literature

Many great names in literature were German speakers. Their stories still resonate today and many of them have been adapted for television and movies. Their works for the stage still appear throughout the world, and they continue to influence the writers of today.

Johann Wolfgang von Goethe

Lived: 1749-1832

Bio: Goethe is one of the most famous authors and poets of the German language, in addition to a noted artist and scientist. He was born in Frankfurt, Germany and traveled extensively throughout his life. He was one of the early writers associated with the Sturm and Drang (Storm and Drive) movement, which creates works of art in which the subjects showed great extremes in emotion.

He wrote not only poetry and novels, but also plays, including the famous, Faust, in which a philosopher makes a pact with the devil.

Many of Goethe's works have been set to music by the likes of Ludwig van Beethoven, Franz Schubert, Johannes Brahms and Gustav Mahler, and he influenced many German authors after him such as Friedrich Nietzsche, Hermann Hesse and Thomas Mann. He also maintained a friendship throughout his life with the famous German playwright Friedrich Schiller, and they are sometimes depicted together in monuments and paintings in their honor.

His wrote poetry of all sorts with vivid images, and often told stories through his poetry, including the ballade on which Disney's The Sorcerer's Apprentice was based.

Famous Works: Faust, the Sorrows of Young Werther, Prometheus, Wilhelm Meister's Apprenticeship, The Sorcerer's Apprentice.

Thomas Mann

Lived: 1875-1955

Bio: Thomas Mann was a German novelist who won the Nobel Prize in literature in 1929. He is best known for his novels that symbolic or ironic nature. He drew on the rich heritage of German literature that had come before him and expanded on the ideas of such authors as Goethe and Nietzsche as well as traditional German tales and biblical accounts.

Famous Works: Buddenbrooks, The Magic Mountain, Death in Venice

Bertolt Brecht

Lived: 1898-1956

Bertolt was a German known for his plays and poetry. He both wrote and directed plays, and even ran a theater company with his wife called the Berliner Ensemble. He lived all over Europe and in the United States. Many of his plays were meant to foster political discussion and shed light on the unjustices of the world. Several of his plays, including his famous Threepenny Opera with which he worked on with famous composer Kurt Weill, have been made into movies.

Famous Works: The Threepenny Opera, Life of Galileo, Mother Courage and Her Children, The Good Person of Szechwan, The Caucasian Chalk Circle, The Resistible Rise of Arturo Ui

Friedrich Nietzsche

Lived: 1844 – 1900

Bio: Friedrich was a famous German philosopher and poet who wrote on such topics such as morality, modern culture, science, and religion. Some of main points were that people had sought to replace God with technology and secularism, that the main drive of mankind is the will to exert strength on the outside world, and the abilty of man to become more than he is.

Famous Works: Thus Spoke Zarathustra, Beyond Good and Evil, The Will to Power, Twilight of the Idols, The Gay Science

Johann Christoph Friedrich von Schiller

Lived: 1759 – 1805

Bio: Friedrich was a famoust German poet and playwright who was a good friend another great German writer, Johann Wolfgang von Goethe. Their often discussed their works and influenced each other. His plays always cast light on the society in which he lived, and many were based on historical events, such as Maria Stuart, which tells the tragic story of Mary, Queen of Scotts. Together with Goethe, he founded the Weimar Theater,w hich heped lead to new interest for drama in Germany.

Many of his poems have been set to music by composers such as Beethoven, Brahms and Schubert. Perhaps the most famous is his poem "An die Freude" or "Ode to Joy", which was used in the final movement of Beethoven's Ninth Symphony. This song is now the official hymn of the United Nations.

Schiller's tweleve remaining plays continue to be popular throughout German-speaking Europe and beyond.

Famous Works: Kabale und Liebe, Die Räuber, An die Freude, Don Carlos, Maria Stuart, Wilhelm Tell

Name: Gotthold Ephraim Lessing

Lived: 1729 - 1781

Bio: Gotthold was a famous German philosopher and writer, who represented the Enlightenment era. He studied many professions, such as a librarian, before finally dedicating himself to the theater. He

admired Shakespeare and wrote works in a similar style. Many of his plays show the need for tolerance between races and religions, especialy in his play, Nathan the Wise, where he showed that Jews, Christians and Muslims should be treated equally. His plays are still often performed.

Famous Works: Nathan der Weise, Minna von Barnhelm, Emilia Galotti

Hermann Hesse

Lived: 1877 - 1962

Bio: The Glass Bead Game, Demian, Steppenwolf, Siddhartha

Famous Works: Hermann was a Swiss German author who won the Nobel Prize in Literature. Both of his parents served Christian missionaries in India, which influenced his later writings. While working in a bookshop, he studied the works of Schiller, Goethe and Nietzche, among others, and decided to become a writer himself. He often spoke against violence, especially against the Nazis.

Wihelm Busch

Lived: 1832-1908

Bio: Wilhelm was a famous German writer and artist, who is known as the "Grandfather of Comics". His children's classic "Max and Moritz" is still a favorite today. It talks about two mischevious children who play pranks on the other people in the town, and whose mischief comes back to bite them in the end. Many of his sayings have become popular idioms.

Famous Works: Max and Moritz

Annette von Droste-Hülshoff

Lived: 1797-1848

Bio: Annette was a famous writer and composer. She and her sister contributed tales to the Grimm Brothers' collection of fairy tales, and Annette decided she wanted to write her own tales. She wrote poetry on various topics, including religious themes and the beauty of nature.

Famous Works: Die Judenbuche

Joseph von Eichendorff

Lived: 1788-1857

Joseph was a famous German poet and novelist of the Romantic period. He came from a noble family and studied law at Heidelberg University. He fought against Napoleon in the Prussian War of Liberation in 1813. In his works, he spoke of the need for a spiritual, rather than political solution to the problems of mankind, and that man could find happiness in immersing himself in nature.

Famous Works: Das Schloss Dürande, Robert Guiscard, Ahnung und Gegenwart, Aus dem Leben eines Taugenichts, das Marmorbild

The Brothers Grimm

Lived: 1785 – 1863, 1786 – 1859

The brothers, Jacob and Wilhelm Grimm were authors born in Hanau Germany. They are most famous for their collection of old folk and fairy tales. Their compilation of tales from all over German-speaking Europe, Children's and Household Tales, was first published in 1812.

Linguists and researchers by trade; they devoted much of their lives to collecting tales from both common people and ancient writings. Timeless fairy tales like Snow White, Cinderella, Little Red Riding Hood, The Princess and the Frog, Hansel and Gretel, Rumpelstizkin, or Rapunzel– to name just a few – have been adapted into other books and movies from the Grimm Brothers' work.

In contrast to the "Disney versions" of these beloved

fairy tales, the original Grimm's tales were often much darker and more violent. Thes tales were originally intended for adults rather than only children.

Thus, the Disney version of Snow White never tells you that the wicked stepmother was invited to attend Snow White's wedding and then forced to dance in heated iron shoes until she died, or that ravens swooped in and pecked out the eyes of Cinderrella's wicked stepmother and sisters. Nor is it common knowledge that in the original Grimm version of The Princess and the Frog that the frog's spell was not broken by a kiss, but when the princess threw it against a wall in disgust.

Their tales and media based on them remain popular to this day.

Famous Works: Kinder und Hausmärchen

E.T.A. Hoffmann

Lived: 1776-1822

Bio: Ernst was a famous Romantic German author and musician, who wrote mostly fantasy and horror. He wrote the novella called The Nutcracker and the Mouse King, one which the ballet The Nutcracker is based. He also wrote for newspapers, and was a noted music critic.

Famous Works: The Nutcracker and the Mouse King, Ritter Gluck, Lebensansichten des Katers Murr, Undine

Karl May

Lived: 1842-1912

Bio: Karl was a famous German author, famous for his adventure novels about the American Old West, the Orient and the Middle East. Many of his works have been turned into movies, stage plays, audio dramas, and comics. He never visited the places he wrote about until much later in his life, though he drew in readers with his strong imagination.

Famous Works: The Winnetou Books

Walter von der Vogelweide

Lived: 1179-1230

Walther was a celebrated German poet, who wrote in what is known as Middle High German, a precursor of modern German. He was a knight, whose name means "Sir Walter of the Bird-Field". He wandered between royal courts, writing and performing lyric poetry to support himself. His poetry sometimes expressed unsually strong political and religious views for the time, though most of it concerned love.

Famous Works: Unter der linden

Michael Ende

Lived: 1929-1995

Michael was a famous German author of children's and fantasy literature. His is best known for his novel "The Neverending Story", which has been made into a series of movies. His works have been translated into dozens of languages and have sold well over 20 million copies.

Famous Works: The Neverending Story, Momo, Jim Button, Luke the Engine Driver.

Anne Frank

Lived: 1929-1945

Anne was a German-born Jewish girl who lived most of her life in the Netherlands. Her family fled Germany after Hitler came to power and hid in a secret annex of an office building for two years to avoid being taken to a concentration camp by the Nazis. During this time, Anne kept a journal describing her confinement, which was later found and translated into many languages as "Dairy of a Young Girl".

Anne's family was betrayed and taken to concentration camps. Anne and her sister Margo died of disease only weeks before Allied troops arrived to liberate them. Today, several plays and movies have been made about Anne's life based on the diary she kept.

Famous Works: Diary of a Young Girl

Vocabulary: On the Phone

Nouns:

German	English
das Telefon	the telephone
der Klingelton	the ringtone
das Handy	the cell phone
der Anruf	the call
der Gruß	the greeting
das R-Gespräch	the collect call
das Ferngespräch	the long-distance call
die Vorwahl	the area code
der Anrufbeantworter	the answering machine
die Textmeldung/SMS	the text message
die besetzte Leitung	the busy line
das Telefonbuch	the phone book
die Nachricht	the voice message

Verbs:

German	English
anrufen	to call on the phone

German	English
sprechen	to speak
reden	to talk
aufheben	to pick up
auflegen	to hang up
warten	to wait
faxen	to send a fax
simsen	to text
stören	to bother
vermissen	to miss someone
einladen	to invite

Phrases:

German	**English**
Ich bin's.	It's me.
Hallo, hier spricht…	Hello, this is
Am Apparat.	Speaking.
Einen Anruf entgegennehmen	to take a call
Darf ich ____ sprechen?	May I speak to…
Kann ich ____ sprechen?	Can I speak to…
Einen Augenblick, bitte.	A moment, please.

Soll ich etwas ausrichten?	Can I take a message.
Danke für den Anruf.	Thank you for your call.
Er/Sie ist nicht da.	He/She is not here.

Unit 24

Grammar: Subjunctive II

Subjunctive is not a case like accusative and dative, but rather a mood, or way of speaking. It does not change any articles or nouns, only verbs.

There are two kinds of subjunctive forms in German. Subjunctive II is sometimes called past subjunctive, because it is formed with the past tense of verbs. Even though it is called past subjunctive, it can be used in any tense.

It is a form that is used to say things that are "contrary to fact", to express something politely, or to express doubt. It is comparable to adding the word would to the verb. I would go, I would like, etc. The verb möchten is actually a subjunctive II form of the word mögen, which is used to sound polite, instead of using wollen.

To create the subjunctive II, take the simple past form and add an –e for singular forms and –en for plural forms. Then, add an umlaut if the verbs contains the vowels a, o, or u (Both sollen and wollen do not taken an umlaut). Let's look at a few examples.

Simple Past	Subjunctive II
ich hatte	ich hätte
du hattest	du hättest
er/sie/es hatte	er/sie/es hätte
wir hatten	wir hätten
ihr hattet	ihr hättet
sie/Sie hatten	sie/Sie hätten

Simple Past	Subjunctive II
ich konnte	ich könnte
du konntest	du könntest
er/sie/es konnte	er/sie/es könnte
wir konnten	wir könnten
ihr konntet	ihr könntet
sie/Sie konnten	sie/Sie könnten

In modern German, the only verbs commonly used in subjunctive II are haben, sein and modal verbs. You should at least know how to form it with other verbs, because sometimes you will hear people use this form with such verbs as **kommen** and **gehen**. For all other verbs, use the subjunctive II form of werden (würden) + the infinitive form of the verb.

Simple Past	**Subjunctive II**
ich war	ich wäre
du warst	du wärst
er/sie/es war	er/sie/es wäre
wir waren	wir wären
ihr wart	ihr wärt
sie/Sie waren	sie/Sie wären

Simple Past	**Subjunctive II**
ich wurde	ich würde
du wurdest	du würdest
er/sie/es wurde	er/sie/es würde
wir wurden	wir würden
ihr wurdet	ihr würdet
sie/Sie wurden	sie/Sie würden

See how this works by looking at some examples of subjunctive II sentences.

German

Ich würde es kaufen, wenn ich mehr Geld hätte.

Er wäre gern mit euch gegangen.

Sie möchte ein Brötchen.

Ich ginge, wenn ich mehr Zeit hätte.

Ich würde gehen, wenn ich mehr Zeit hätte.

English

I would buy it if I had more money.

I would have liked to go with you all.

She would like a roll.

I would go if I had more time.

I would go if I had more time.

Pronunciation: The Letter Y

The letter Y does not show up very often in German. Usually, you will only see it in foreign words which are borrowed into German. Many of these words are from English and be spelled with either a Y or by using a J instead. Here are some examples.

German	English
das Yoyo	the yoyo
die Yacht	the yacht

There are some German words that use Y and it sounds like a U Umlaut. Some of these words have been borrowed from Greek. Here are some examples.

German	English
das Gymnasium	the secondary school
die Hymne	the hymn

Another common word you will see with Y is ***das Handy***, which means *cell phone*.

Culture: German Music

Almost everyone knows names like Beethoven, Bach and Mozart, but did you know that they were all German speakers? Many famous composers were born and worked in German-speaking countries, especially Germany and Austria. The capital city of Austria, Vienna (Wien) has historically been one of the most important cities for western music in the world, and still remains an important cultural center. Here are some composers you might want to look up, including a little bit about each one, and some of their most famous works.

Johann Sebastian Bach

Lived: 1685-1750 AD

Bio: Bach was one of the most famous composers of the Baroque Period. He is most known for his works for organ of which he was a master. He also wrote choral, orchestral and piano works that are often performed today. Many of his works showcase the method of counterpoint, which involves having multiple complimentary melodies being played a once.

He was born in Eisenach, Germany into a family that was already musical. He learned various instruments from his family members growing up, including the harpsichord (the precursor of the piano) and the violin. He studied After studying at St. Michael's School in Lüneburg, he went on to hold important posts, such as a director of music to Prince Leopold of Köthen, Cantor of Thomasschule in Leipzig and the Royal Court Composer to August III. Unlike many other famous composers, Bach never traveled far from the city of his birth.

Many of Bach's compositions were not recognized in his lifetime, but came into the public's consciousness during a revival of interest in his works during the 19th century. He is widely regarded as one of the greatest composers of all time.

Famous works: Jesu Bleibet Meine Freude (Jesu, Joy of Man's Desiring), Tocatta and Fugue in D minor, Brandenburg Concertos, Mass in B, The Well-Tempered Clavier, The Art of Fugue, St. Matthew's Passion, Ein feste Burg ist unser Gott

(Choral), Wachet auf, ruft uns die Stimme, Herz und Mund und Tag und Leben

Wolfgang Amadeus Mozart

Lived: 27 Jan 1756 – 5 Dec 1791

Bio: Mozart is known as one of the most influential and prolific composers of the Classical era of music, even though he did not live a long life. He was seen as a musical Wunderkind or child prodigy and composed his own music, some of which was performed for royalty, starting at age five. No one knows for sure why he died at such a young age, leaving behind a wife, Constanze, and two sons.

His middle name "Amadeus" was not his given middle name, but one that he applied to himself. It is Latin for "beloved of God."

He was born and did much of his work in Salzburg, Austria. He also spent much of his time in the Austrian capital city, Vienna. In his life, he wrote over 600 works, and had a profound influence on those who came after him, including Ludwig van Beethoven.

Famous works: Die Zauberflöte (The Magic Flute), Don Giovanni, The Marriage of Figaro, Requiem in D Minor,

Ludwig Van Beethoven

Lived: 1770-1827 AD

Bio: Ludwig van Beethoven is one of the most admired, influential and revolutionary German composers ever. Born in Bonn, Germany, to a large family with a rich musical heritage, Beethoven began to be taught by his father at a young age to

play the piano. Though he was no child prodigy like Mozart, Beethoven grew steadily in his musical talent and now is known as one of the giants of classical music.

In his early 20's, he moved to Vienna and studied with Joseph Haydn, who was a well-known composer of symphonies, and was soon discovered as a brilliant composer and piano virtuoso. One of the most well-known facts about Beethoven is probably his hearing loss that began in 1795 and worsened over the years until his complete deafness around 1819. It is said that at the end of the premiere of his famous Ninth Symphony, he had to be turned around to see the tumultuous applause of the audience and hearing nothing, he wept.

He had written this entire symphony and many of his other works without the aid of hearing. He suffered for poor health generally, and sometimes considered committing suicide, but decided against it, because of the music he still wished to bring out of his mind.

His illness prevented him from performing and conducting and made him distance himself from others, but it did not keep him from composing. In addition to numerous other compositions, Beethoven created nine symphonies, 16 compositions for string quartets and 32 piano sonatas. He is also regarded as a vital link between the Classical and Romantic movements of music.

Famous works: Fifth Symphony, Ninth Symphony (An die Freude/Ode to Joy), Moonlight Sonata, Für Elise, Pathetique sonata, Op. 13, Fidelio, Missa Solemnis

Georg Friedrich Handel

Lived: 1685 - 1759

Bio: Though Handel was born in Halle, Germany, he did most of his work in other countries, including England, and became a British subject in 1727. He also spent time in Italy and was heavily influenced by both German and Italian composers. Near the end of his life, he was nearly blind, but died having gained wealth and respect in his lifetime unlike composers such as Johann Sebastian Bach.

Handel wrote both instrumental and choral music, in addition to 29 oratorios and 42 operas. He often wrote for royalty and so some of his works were done for events such as royal coronations and weddings.

One of his most famous works is probably the oratorio Messiah, from which the Hallelujah Chorus is taken. Most of the text comes from the King James Bible and it was first performed in Dublin, Ireland in 1742. It tells of the life of Jesus Christ, starting with the prophesies of His coming, and then discussing His life, death and resurrection. The entire work was composed in only 24 days after which he wrote the inscription "SDG" which represent the Latin words Soli Deo Gloria—To God alone the glory.

It is a common custom for audiences to stand during the Hallelujah Chorus.

Famous works: Water Music, Music for the Royal Fireworks, Messiah

Johannes Brahms

Lived: 1833 - 1897

Bio: Johannes was a German composer who spent much of his life in Vienna. Unlike some other composers like Bach, Brahams was popular during his lifetime. He produced music for a variety of ensembles, including piano, orchestra, and choruses. His experize in the piano meant that he showcases many of his own works.

He wrote four symphonies, piano and organ pieces, many concertos for various instruments and even a large choral requiem that broke from the traditional style of requiems at the time. A traditional requiem set religious texts in Latin to music. Brahams, however, chose his own selections from the Lutheran Bible, which resulted in a requiem with a more positive tone that many others.

His compositions have proven of lasting value and are still commonly performed by modern ensembles. Part of his appeal likely lies that he did composed some music traditional for the time, but also so that was ahead of its time, all with excellent technique.

Famous works: Ein Deutsches Requiem, Brahms's Lullaby, Hungarian Dances

Franz Schubert

Lived: 1797 - 1828

Bio: Though Schubert only lifved for 32 years, he wrote over 600 pieces of music, including nine symphonies, piano music, operas and choral music.

His works grew in popularity after his death, starting later in the 19th centure and continuing to today. He is considered to be one of the earliest Romantic composers. Schubert worked mostly in Vienna and died there of typhoid fever in 1828. On his death bed, he requested a friend play a string piece by Beethoven. Schubert admired Beethoven all his life and was buried next to him at his own request.

Famous works: Der Erlkönig, Die Forelle, Die schöne Müllerin, Winterreise,

Richard Strauss

Lived: 1864 - 1949

Bio: Richard was a German composer of the late Romantic period who was especially known for his operas. In addition to composing, he directed music throughout the German-speaking world.

He learned the musical arts from his father and wrote his first composition at age six. He did not stop writing music until shortly before his death. While still young, he saw a few of Richard Wagners epic operas, and these profoundly inspired him.

Though he was appointed the head of the State Music Beueru during the Third Reich, he bitterly opposed the views of the Nazis and tried to continue performances of music by banned composers such as Mendelssohn and Debussy, and his collaboration with Jewish composers. His opposition resulted in his lose of his position, though they still used his Olympic Hymn for the Berlin 1936 Summer Olympics.

He is said to have taken the position in the first place to keep some of his Jewish relatives from being taken to camps.

Strauss lived a long life and left a legacy of remarkable music.

Famous works: Der Rosenkavalier, Salome, Death and Transfiguration, Till Eulenspiegel's Merry Pranks, Also Sprach Zarathustra, An Alpine Symphony, Metamorphosen

Franz Joseph Haydn

Lived: 1732 - 1809

Bio: Joseph was an Austrian composer, and one of the most famous composers of the Classical period. He developed the nickname "Father of the Symphony", because he wrote so many, and set the standard for other composers to follow.

He spent much of his career as the court musican for a wealthy family, the Esterhazys. They lived on a remote estate, so that he was cut off from other composers for most of his life, and thus forced to constantly come up with new kinds of music. He often included humorous surpised in his music, such as sudden changes in dynamics that listeners did not expect.

He was a friend of Mozart and one of Beethoven's

teachers.

Famous works: The Creation, The Seasons, Trauer Symphony No. 44, Farewell Symphony No. 45, Surprise Symphony

Richard Wagner

Lived: 1813 - 1883

Bio: Richard Wagner (1813-1883) was a famous German composer, director, and conductor, mostly known for his operas. Wagner is well known for his love of recurring themes or Leitmotive. This inspired many modern film composers to craft recurring themes for characters in their movies. Many popular movies, such as Star Wars and Lord of the Rings, use recurring musical themes for their characters.

Much of his music was radical and experimental for the time, and many of his ideas have been further developed in modern music. He wrote his operas to be a "Gesamtkunstwerk" or "total work of art", that was meant to bring all the arts together, such as poetry, visual arts, musical arts, dramtic arts, etc.

Some of his most recognized operas or music dramas are The Flying Dutchman, Tristan und Isolde and Percival (Parzival). Wagner received world fame for his extensive epic work, The Ring of the Nibelung (Ring des Nibelungen). A section from his opera, Lohengrin, called the "Bridal Chorus" is often played for weddings in English-speaking countries.

To better be able to perform his works, Richard Wagner, had his own opera house build in Bayreuth, Germany, later known as the Bayreuth Festspielhaus. Every year thousands of people come from all over the world to watch and listen to the spectacular Bayreuth Festival that is still carried on by his descendants.

Famous works: Tristian und Isolde, der Fliegende Hollander, Der Ring des Nibelungen, die Meistersinger von Nürnberg, Tannhäuser, Lohengrin, Parsifal, the Bridal Chorus

Hildegard von Bingen

Lived: 1098 - 1179

Bio: Hildegard was a Catholic Saint and was a German writer, physician, artist, and composer. She founded monasteries in Germany and wrote musical presentations for those who lived their. Her works included some of the earliest-known liturgical dramas and morality plays, which are dramatic reperentation meant to teach religious concepts to the audience.

About seventy of her music compositions have survived, each with poetic texts. Her music was monophonic, meaning that it had only one melody line, and her melodies were often more complex than others to her time.

Famous works: Ordo Virtutum, Dendermonde, Riesenkodex

Felix Mendelssohn

Lived: 1809 - 1847

Bio: Felix Mendelssohn was a German composer, conductor, and musican, recognized in his early childhood as a musical prodigy. Though he came from a Jewish family, he was later baptized a Lutheran. He traveled through all of Europe and he was especially well-loved in England. He brought new interest to the works of Johann Sebastian Bach and was not as radical as some of his contemporaries, such as Wagner, Liszt, and Berlioz.

He wrote symphonies, oratorios, piano music, and

choir music, among other things in the Romantic style. One of his important works he composed is the "Wedding March" that is traditionally played at a weddings, paired with Richard Wagner's "Bridal Chorus".

Because Mendelssohn came from a Jewish family, his works were forbidden or made unfashionable in Germany and other countries for a time, especially by the Third Reich. These days, however, his works have regained their popularity.

Famous works: The Wedding March, A Midsummer Night's Dream, the Italian Symphony, Eijah, St. Paul, Scottish Symphony

Carl Orff

Lived: 1895 - 1982

Bio: Carl was a 20th century German composer and educator who developed a new approach for teaching music to children. He is best known for his cantata called Carmina Burana, which is based on medival German poetry. Music from this cantata is often featured in modern movie trailers or TV commericals.

He wrote musical lessons called Schulwerk, intended to teach school children about different musical concepts. His methods are still used today and include singing, playing instruments (especially keyboard or xylophone-like instruments) movement, and improvisation.

Famous works: Carmina Burana, Der Mond, Die Kluge, Antigonae, De Temporum Fine Comoedia

Johann Pachelbel

Lived: 1653 - 1706

Bio: Johann was a German composer and organist of the Baroque period. He wrote a large variety of both secular and sacred music, and enjoyed great popularity during his lifetime. His Cannon in D or "Pachabel's Cannon" as it is sometimes known, has enjoyed special popularity through time and can still often be heard today.

Famous works: Cannon in D, Chaconne in F minor, Hexachordum

Robert and Clara Schumann

Lived: 1810 - 1856

Bio: Robert was one of the great German composers of the Romatic period. He originally intended to make a career as a pianst, but experienced a severe hand injury and so instead set to work on composing. He first focused only on piano compositions, but later in life wrote for orchestras, choirs and other small groups. He founded a music magazine in Leipzig called "die Neue Zeitschift für Musik". He wrote extensively as a music critic in this magazine. He married Clara, Wieck, the daughter of his former music teacher. She not only composed many of her own songs, but also enjoyed a successful concert career.

Famous works: Carnaval, Op. 9, Fantasiestücke, Davidsbündlertänze, Op.6, Kinderszenen, Op. 15, Kreisleriana

Johann Strauss II

Lived: 1825 – 1899

Bio: Both Johann and his father Johann, Sr. were notable Austrian composers, known for composing "light music", such as dances and operettas. He is sometimes known as "the Waltz King", because of his mastery of writing waltzes, which at the time, were extremely popular in Vienna. Johann's father, also a gifted composer, did not want to his son to become a musican, but Johann secretly studied the violin with the first violist of his father's orchestra. His father eventually left their family, and Johann continued as a musican with the support of his mother.

Famous Works: The Blue Danube, Tritsch-Tratsch, Die Fledermaus, Der Zigeunerbaron

Gustav Mahler

Lived: 1860 – 1911

Bio: Gustav was an Austrian composer of the late Romantic period. His music bridged the gap between the traditional music of the 19th century and the newer modern music of the 20th century. Because of his Jewish heritigage, his music was banned by the Nazis, but then rediscovered after the war, and is still frequently performed.

In addition to composing, Gustav was one of the most well-known conductors of his time and traveled the world on a rigorous schedule.

Famous Works: Das Lied von der Erde, Kindertotenlieder, Symphonies 1-9

Arnold Schönberg

Lived: 1874 - 1951

Bio: Arnold was an Austrian composer who created a whole new way of thinking about music. Instead of using traditional compositional methods, Arnold used what is called the twelve-tone technique, which creates music that can sound dissonant and strange to some. Wihle some denounced his kind of music, others, such as composers Alban Berg and Anton Webern, learned from him and turned Arnolds techniques into a full-blown movement.

Famous Works: Verklärte Nacht, Pelleas und Melisande, Frieden auf Erden, 15 Gedichte aus Das Buch der hängenden Gärten, Pierrot lunaire, Op. 21

Vocabulary: Professions

Nouns:

(Note: Most profession nouns can be changed from male to female by changing der to die and adding – in to the end. Sometimes you have to add an umlaut as well, such as der Arzt, die Ärztin.)

German	English
der Beruf	the profession
das Gehalt	the salary
der Chef	the boss
die Arbeit	the work
das Geld	the money
das Büro	the office
der Schreibtisch	the desk
der Angestellte	the employee (male)
die Angestellte	the employee (female)
der Arbeitgeber	the employer
die Versammlung	the meeting
der Buchhalter	the accountant
der Architekt	the architect

der Künstler	the artist
der Sportler	the athelete
der Geschäftsmann	the businessman
die Geschäftsfrau	the businesswoman
der Zahnarzt	the dentist
der Tierarzt	the veterinarian
der Bauer	the farmer
der Feuerwehrmann	the firefighter
der Richter	the judge
der Anwalt	the lawyer
der Postbote	the mail carrier
der Mechaniker	the mechanic
der Arzt	the doctor
die Krankenschwester	the female nurse
der Krankenpfleger	the male nurse
der Maler	the painter
der Klempner	the plumber
der Polizist	the police officer
der Politiker	the politician

der Wissenschaftler	the scientist
der Sänger	the singer
der Lehrer	the teacher
der Professor	the professor
der Kellner	the waiter
der Schriftsteller	the writer
der Schauspieler	the actor
der Archäologe	the archaeologist
der Metzger	the butcher
der Tischler	the carpenter
der Trainer	the coach
der Flugbegleiter	the flight attendant
der Journalist	the journalist
der Gärtner	the gardner
der Bürgermeister	the mayor
der Musiker	the musician
der Maler	the painter
der Fotograf	the photographer
der Pilot	the pilot

der Verkäufer	the salesman
der Chirurg	the surgeon
der Übersetzer	the translator
der Ingenieur	the engineer
der Astronaut	the astronaut
der Flughafen	the airport
der Pfarrer	the pastor
die Bäckerei	the bakery
die Bank	the bank
die Kirche	the church
die Turnhalle	the gym
die Fabrik	the factory
der Friseur	the hair salon
die Eisdiele	the ice cream shop
die Bibliothek	the library
das Kino	the movie theater
das Museum	the museum
die Apotheke	the pharmacy
die Post	the post office

das Restaurant	the restaurant
das Stadion	the stadium
der Laden	the store
der Markt	the market
das Theater	the theater
die Universität	the university
das Café	the café
das Rathaus	the city hall

Verbs:

German	English
arbeiten	to work
verdienen	to earn
entlassen	to fire/let go
feuern	to fire
probieren	to try
lernen	to learn
studieren	to study
eine Stelle bekommen	to get a job

Phrases:

German	English
Was machen Sie beruflich?	What do you do for a job?
Was studieren Sie?	What are you studying?

Common Questions and Answers

The following is a list of common questions that missionaries are asked and some common answers for you practice in German. These are not the only responses possible, and you should remember to always answer in the way that the Spirit directs. These are meant as suggestions only.

- Do Mormons believe in Christ?

Yes, he is our Savior.

Yes, the actual name of our church is the Church of Jesus Christ of Latter-day Saints.

Glauben Mormonen an Christus?

Ja, er ist unser Erlöser.

Ja, der eigentliche Name unserer Kirche ist die Kirche Jesu Christi der Heiligen der Letzten Tage.

- Do Mormons believe in the Bible?

Yes, we believe that it is the word of God.

Yes, and also the Book of Mormon. They are both important.

Glauben Mormonen an die Bibel?

Ja, wir glauben, dass sie das Wort Gottes ist.

Ja, und auch an das Buch Mormon. Sie sind beide

wichtig.

- Are you Jehovah's Witnesses/Mennonites?

No, but we are missionaries, and reprentatives of Jesus Christ.

Sind Sie Zeugen Jehovahs/Mennoniten?

Nein, aber wir sind Missionare und Vertreter Jesu Christi.

- Are you a sect?

No, we are a part of the Church of Jesus Christ.

No, but we are not Catholic or Lutheran.

Sind Sie eine Sekte?

Nein, wir sind ein Teil der Kirche Jesu Christi.

Nein, aber wir sind weder Katholisch noch Evangelisch.

- Are you only an American church?

No, we have members throughout the world.

No, there are more members outside of the United States than inside.

Sind Sie nur eine Amerikanische Kirche?

Nein, wir haben Mitglieder in der ganzen Welt.

Nein, es gibt mehr Mitglieder ausserhalbe der Vereinigten Staaten als innerhalb.

- Why don't Mormons drink tee/coffee/alcohol?

The things can harm the body.

It is a commandment of God through a prophet.

Warum trinken Mormonen keinen Kaffee/Tee/Alkohol?

Diese Sachen schaden dem Körper.

Es ist ein Gebot Gottes durch einen Propheten.

- Don't you worship Joseph Smith?

We respect Joseph Smith, but worship Jesus Christ.

Joseph Smith was a great prophet, but not equal to Jesus.

Beten Sie Joseph Smith nicht an?

Wir ehren Joseph Smith, aber beten Jesus Christus an.

Joseph Smith war ein grosser Prophet, aber war nicht Jesus gleich.

- Don't Mormons have many wives?

In the past, a few members had more than one

wife.

Church members are no longer allowed to have more than one wife.

Haben Mormonen nicht viele Frauen?

In der Vergangenheit, hatten manche Mitglieder mehr als eine Frau.

Kirchenmitglieder dürfen jetzt nicht mehr als eine Frau haben.

- Why are you here?

We are here to share a message.

We are here to represent Jesus Christ.

We are here to serve.

Warum sind Sie hier?

Wir sind hier um eine Botschaft mitzuteilen.

Wir sind hier um Jesus Christus zu vertreten.

Wir sind hier um zu dienen.

Why are there so many bad people on the earth?

God gives us all the choice between good and evil. He will not take that away.

The influence of Satan is real, but he will lose in the end.

Warum gibt es so viele schlechte Menschen auf Erden?

Gott gibt uns allen die Entscheidung zwischen Gut und Böse. Er wird sie nicht wegnehmen.

Der Einfluss Satans ist real, aber er wird am Ende verlieren.

Why can't we simply follow the Pope?

Today, there is a living prophet on the earth.

Warum können wir nicht einfach dem Papst folgen?

Es gibt heute einen lebendigen Propheten auf Erden.

Why is a church so important when faith is such a personal thing?

We need more than faith to be saved. We need holy ordinances.

When faithful people come together, they strengthen each other.

Warum ist eine Kirche so wichtig wenn der Glauben etwas persönliches ist?

Wir brauchen mehr als den Glauben, um errettet zu werden. Wir brauchen auch heilige Handlungen.

Wenn glaubensvolle Menschen

zusammenkommen, stärken sie einander.

Priesthood Ordinances in German and English

The following guidelines are taken from the LDS Handbook 2: Administering in the Church and from the scriptures:

Anleitung für die Namensgebung und Kindessegnung - Deutsch

1. Er ruft den Vater im Himmel an.

2. Er sagt, dass diese Segnung kraft der Vollmacht des Melchisedekischen Priestertums vollzogen wird.

3. Er gibt dem Kind einen Namen.

4. Er fügt Segensworte hinzu, wie der Geist ihn leitet.

5. Er schließt im Namen Jesu Christi.

Instructions for Naming and Blessing a Child – English

1. Addresses Heavenly Father.

2. States that the blessing is performed by the authority of the Melchizedek Priesthood.

3. Gives the child a name.

4. Gives words of blessing as the Spirit directs.

5. Closes in the name of Jesus Christ.

Die Taufe – Deutsch

1. Er stellt sich mit dem Täufling ins Wasser.

2. Er fasst mit seiner linken Hand das rechte Handgelenk des Täuflings (aus Sicherheitsgründen und weil es so einfacher ist); dann ergreift der Täufling mit der linken Hand das linke Handgelenk des Täufers.

3. Er hebt den rechten Arm rechtwinklig.

4. Er nennt den Täufling beim vollen Namen und sagt: „Beauftragt von Jesus Christus, taufe ich dich im Namen des Vaters und des Sohnes und des Heiligen Geistes. Amen." (LuB 20:73.)

5. Er lässt den Täufling sich mit der rechten Hand die Nase zuhalten (damit es angenehmer ist), legt seine rechte Hand oben auf den Rücken des Täuflings und taucht ihn mitsamt der Kleidung vollständig unter.

6. Er hilft dem Täufling wieder aus dem Wasser.

Baptism – English

1. Stands in the water with the person to be

baptized.

2. Holds the person's right wrist with his left hand (for convenience and safety); the person who is being baptized holds the priesthood holder's left wrist with his or her left hand.

3. Raises his right arm to the square.

4. States the person's full name and says, "Having been commissioned of Jesus Christ, I baptize you in the name of the Father, and of the Son, and of the Holy Ghost. Amen" (D&C 20:73).

5. Has the person hold his or her nose with the right hand (for convenience); then the priesthood holder places his right hand high on the person's back and immerses the person completely, including the person's clothing.

6. Helps the person come up out of the water.

Die Konfirmierung

1. Er nennt den Betreffenden beim vollen Namen.

2. Er sagt, dass die heilige Handlung kraft der Vollmacht des Melchisedekischen Priestertums vollzogen wird.

3. Er bestätigt den Betreffenden als Mitglied der

Kirche Jesu Christi der Heiligen der Letzten Tage.

4. Er verwendet die Worte: „Empfange den Heiligen Geist" (nicht: „Empfange die Gabe des Heiligen Geistes").

5. Er fügt Segensworte hinzu, wie der Geist ihn leitet.

6. Er schließt im Namen Jesu Christi.

Confirmation – English

1. States the person's full name.

2. States that the ordinance is performed by the authority of the Melchizedek Priesthood.

3. Confirms the person a member of The Church of Jesus Christ of Latter-day Saints.

4. Uses the words "Receive the Holy Ghost" (not "receive the gift of the Holy Ghost").

5. Gives words of blessing as the Spirit directs.

6. Closes in the name of Jesus Christ.

Das Abendmahl - Deutsch

Brot

O Gott, Ewiger Vater, wir bitten dich im Namen deines Sohnes, Jesus Christus, segne und heilige dieses Brot für die Seele all derer, die davon nehmen, damit sie zum Gedächtnis des Leibes deines Sohnes essen und dir, o Gott, Ewiger Vater, bezeugen, daß sie willens sind, den Namen deines Sohnes auf sich zu nehmen und immer an ihn zu denken und seine Gebote, die er ihnen gegeben hat, zu halten, damit sein Geist immer mit ihnen sei. Amen.

Wasser

O Gott, Ewiger Vater, wir bitten dich im Namen deines Sohnes, Jesus Christus, segne und heilige dieses Wasser für die Seele all derer, die davon trinken, damit sie es zum Gedächtnis des Blutes deines Sohnes tun, das für sie vergossen wurde, damit sie dir, o Gott, Ewiger Vater, bezeugen, daß sie wahrhaftig immer an ihn denken, damit sein Geist mit ihnen sei. Amen.

The Sacrament – English

Bread

O God, the Eternal Father, we ask thee in the name of thy Son, Jesus Christ, to bless and sanctify this bread to the souls of all those who partake of it, that they may eat in remembrance of the body of thy Son, and witness unto thee, O God, the Eternal Father, that they are willing to take upon them the name of thy Son, and always remember him and keep his commandments which he has given them; that they may always have his Spirit to be with them. Amen.

Water

O God, the Eternal Father, we ask thee in the name of thy Son, Jesus Christ, to bless and sanctify this water to the souls of all those who drink of it, that they may do it in remembrance of the blood of thy Son, which was shed for them; that they may witness unto thee, O God, the Eternal Father, that they do always remember him, that they may have his Spirit to be with them. Amen.

Die Weihung von Öl

1. Er nimmt das geöffnete Gefäß mit Olivenöl in die Hand.

2. Er ruft den Vater im Himmel an.

3. Er sagt, dass er kraft der Vollmacht des Melchisedekischen Priestertums handelt.

4. Er weiht das Öl (nicht das Gefäß) und bestimmt es für die Salbung und das Segnen von Kranken und Bedrängten.

5. Er schließt im Namen Jesu Christi.

Die Salbung mit Öl – Deutsch

1. Er gibt dem zu Segnenden einen Tropfen geweihten Öls auf den Kopf.

2. Er legt ihm leicht die Hände auf den Kopf und nennt ihn beim vollen Namen.

3. Er sagt, dass er kraft der Vollmacht des Melchisedekischen Priestertums handelt.

4. Er sagt, dass er ihn mit Öl salbt, das zum Salben und Segnen von Kranken und Bedrängten geweiht ist.

5. Er schließt im Namen Jesu Christi.

Consecrating Oil – English

1. Holds an open container of olive oil.

2. Addresses Heavenly Father.

3. States that he is acting by the authority of the Melchizedek Priesthood.

4. Consecrates the oil (not the container) and sets it apart for anointing and blessing the sick and afflicted.

5. Closes in the name of Jesus Christ.

Annointing with Oil -English

1. Puts a drop of consecrated oil on the person's head.

2. Places his hands lightly on the person's head and calls the person by his or her full name.

3. States that he is acting by the authority of the Melchizedek Priesthood.

4. States that he is anointing with oil that has been consecrated for anointing and blessing the sick and afflicted.

5. Closes in the name of Jesus Christ.

Die Siegelung der Salbung -Deutsch

1. Er nennt den Betreffenden beim vollen Namen.

2. Er sagt, dass er die Salbung kraft der Vollmacht des Melchisedekischen Priestertums siegelt.

3. Er fügt Segensworte hinzu, wie der Geist ihn

leitet.

4. Er schließt im Namen Jesu Christi.

Sealing the Anointing - English

1. Calls the person by his or her full name.

2. States that he is sealing the anointing by the authority of the Melchizedek Priesthood.

3. Gives words of blessing as the Spirit directs.

4. Closes in the name of Jesus Christ.

Anleitung, wie eine Ordinierung vollzogen wird – Deutsch

1. Er nennt den Betreffenden beim vollen Namen.

2. Er nennt die Vollmacht (das Aaronische oder das Melchisedekische Priestertum), kraft derer die Ordinierung vollzogen wird.

3. Er überträgt das Aaronische oder Melchisedekische Priestertum, sofern das nicht schon früher geschehen ist.

4. Er ordiniert den Betreffenden zu einem Amt im Aaronischen oder Melchisedekischen Priestertum und überträgt die Rechte und die Macht und

Vollmacht dieses Amtes. (Bei der Übertragung des Priestertums und bei der Ordinierung zu einem dieser Ämter werden keine Priestertumsschlüssel übertragen.)

5. Er fügt Segensworte hinzu, wie der Geist ihn leitet.

6. Er schließt im Namen Jesu Christi.

Instructions for Performing an Ordination - English

1. Calls the person by his full name.

2. States the authority by which the ordination is performed (Aaronic or Melchizedek Priesthood).

3. Confers the Aaronic or Melchizedek Priesthood, unless it has already been conferred.

4. Ordains the person to an office in the Aaronic or Melchizedek Priesthood and bestows the rights, powers, and authority of that office. (Priesthood keys are not bestowed in conferring the priesthood or ordaining to one of these offices.)

5. Gives words of blessing as the Spirit directs.

6. Closes in the name of Jesus Christ.

Die Weihung eines Grabes – Deutsch

1. Er ruft den Vater im Himmel an.

2. Er sagt, dass er kraft der Vollmacht des Melchisedekischen Priestertums handelt.

3. Er weiht die Grabstätte als Ruheplatz für den Leichnam des Verstorbenen.

4. Er betet darum (sofern angemessen), dass diese Stelle bis zur Auferstehung geheiligt und geschützt bleibe.

5. Er bittet den Herrn, er möge die Angehörigen trösten, und fügt hinzu, was der Geist ihm eingibt.

6. Er schließt im Namen Jesu Christi.

Dedicating Graves – English

1. Addresses Heavenly Father.

2. States that he is acting by the authority of the Melchizedek Priesthood.

3. Dedicates and consecrates the burial plot as the resting place for the body of the deceased.

4. Prays that the place will be hallowed and protected until the Resurrection (where appropriate).

5. Asks the Lord to comfort the family and expresses thoughts as the Spirit directs.

6. Closes in the name of Jesus Christ.

Checklist for a Baptism

A baptism is a pivotal point in a person's progression. You should make every effort to ensure that everything runs smoothly. The following is a checklist of things to remember when preparing for a baptismal service.

• Find someone to conduct. (Any member of the ward leadership usually works fine.)

• Find someone to conduct the music.

• Find someone to accompany the music and play prelude and postlude music. If no one is available, arrange for recorded accompaniment if possible.

• Arrange for someone to say the opening and closing prayers.

• Make sure you know who is performing the baptism and confirmation.

• Make sure that the person baptizing and the person being baptized both have white clothing in their size.

• Make sure that the people participating in the ordinance have an extra change of clothes to change into after the baptism.

• Make sure that you have some activity for the time in which the people who participated in the baptism are changing their clothes. This can include a musical number, a short film, or the bearing of testimonies.

• Make sure you know who will be giving at the talks. Traditionally, a baptism includes a talk on the Holy Ghost and a talk on baptism.

• Make sure the building is scheduled during the time in which you wish to perform the baptism.

• Make sure that the baptism is announced in the ward or branches church meetings.

• Make sure that the friends and family of the one being baptized are invited.

• Make sure you have made all of the arrangements for any gatherings after the baptism.

• Make sure the church or other building is left clean and orderly once everyone is done.

• Make sure that the baptismal interview has been performed.

• Make sure that you have to wear the witnesses available to witness the baptism and confirmation.

• Make sure that all the necessary paperwork is in order.

ABOUT THE AUTHOR

Michael is a graduate of Brigham Young University and Western Governors University with degrees in German, Music and Instructional Design. He served an LDS Mission in Frankfurt, Germany.

He puts his education to good use designing and teaching online courses. Though he grew up traveling the world with his military father, he now lives in Utah with his wife, Jen, and his two sons. He enjoys acting in community theater, playing and writing music, and writing fiction.

He played for several years with the handbell choir Bells on Temple Square and is now a member of the Mormon Tabernacle Choir. He is the author of the many books, including *The Canticle Kingdom*, *The Last Archangel*, and *The Song of the Righteous*.

www.ingramcontent.com/pod-product-compliance
Lightning Source LLC
Chambersburg PA
CBHW071028290526
45795CB00004B/1145